The Bilingual Revolution Series

TBR Books

A Program of The Center for the Advancement of Languages, Education, and Communities (CALEC)

Our Books in English

The Gift of Languages: Paradigm Shift in U.S. Foreign Language Education by Fabrice Jaumont and Kathleen Stein-Smith

Two Centuries of French Education in New York: The Role of Schools in Cultural Diplomacy by Jane Flatau Ross

The Clarks of Willsborough Point: The Long Trek North by Darcey Hale

The Bilingual Revolution: The Future of Education is in Two Languages by Fabrice Jaumont

Our Books in Translation

Die bilinguale Revolution: Die Zukunft der Bildung liegt in zwei Sprachen by Fabrice Jaumont

La revolución bilingüe: El futuro de la educación está en dos idiomas by Fabrice Jaumont

ДВУЯЗЫЧНАЯ РЕВОЛЮЦИЯ: БУДУЩЕЕ ОБРАЗОВАНИЯ НА ДВУХ ЯЗЫКАХ by Фабрис Жомон

La Révolution bilingue: Le futur de l'éducation s'écrit en deux langues by Fabrice Jaumont

Other volumes of the trilogy

Mamma in her Village (2019, first published in 2005);

Beyond Gibraltar (2019, first published in 2013).

Other Publications

Edition of Lorenzo Valla's *de Voluptate* (1431-44);

*On Pleasure (*translation of Lorenzo Valla's *de Voluptate);*

A Defense of Life: Lorenzo Valla's Theory of Pleasure;

Folly and Insanity in Renaissance Literature (with Ernesto Grassi);

Edition of Ziliolo Zilioli's *Michaelida* (1431).

THE OTHER SHORE

Maristella de Panizza Lorch

TBR Books is a program of the Center for the Advancement of Languages, Education, and Communities. We publish researchers and practitioners who seek to engage diverse communities on topics related to education, languages, cultural history, and social initiatives.

TBR Books
146 Norman Avenue
Brooklyn, New York
www.tbr-books.org | contact@tbr-books.org

Front Cover Illustration © Greg Rosenke
Cover Design © Eunjoo Feaster

ISBN 978-1-947626-24-9 (paperback)
ISBN 978-1-947626-25-6 (eBook)
Library of Congress Control Number: 2019944291

CONTENTS

Maristella de Panizza Lorch's *The Other Shore* is at one level a love story, chronicling the romance and marriage of two European intellectuals who fled the perils of the old world for an academic sanctuary across the Atlantic. But it is also a lyrical celebration of three distinct cultures—European, American, and African—and of the tight-knit family whose curiosity and peripatetic lives spanned all of them. In narrating her century-long journey, Lorch takes her readers from Nazi-occupied Rome to Columbia University, from a wooded retreat in the Catskill Mountains to a bush camp in the heart of Kenya's Masai Mara. Describing her three daughters' growth into ambitious, independent women, and the courageous struggle of her soul mate of nearly forty years against a fatal illness, she creates a magical tableau of life, literature, and the love that binds a family. What comes through most by the end of this beautiful story is her declaration in a letter to a granddaughter who stands on the cusp of adulthood: "To exist," she proclaims, "means to realize the best of oneself without fear of limits."

—Joshua Hammer, author of *The Bad-Ass Librarians of Timbuktu* (and the upcoming *The Falcon Thief*)

***

There have been a fair number of autobiographical narratives of the great intellectual migration by scientists, artists, humanists and others escaping the horrors of Hitler's Germany and Mussolini's Italy in the 1930s and '40s. But none are quite like this enormously interesting, gripping, and powerful trilogy, *Beyond Gibraltar,* by Maristella Lorch. Her journey from her native town near the border of Italy and Austria, to studies in Rome, to her capture by the Nazis, her escape beyond Gibraltar to New York and the United States, make for a riveting life story. This totally engaging woman is nothing short of a Shavian life force. Initially living in virtual poverty in New York, this

13

accomplished woman found a job at Barnard College and Columbia University and spent the rest of her academic life challenging the orthodoxies of university culture.

Her sheer energy, her unflappable determination, and her powerful intellect made her a revered teacher, a notable Dante scholar, and an academic entrepreneur—who would befriend leaders of the Italian government, the leading directors of cinema and theater in the years after the War, as well as distinguished scholars in her field. The story is one of courage and intellectual and physical vitality. The stage is the world, but a world that returns always to Columbia and her passion for beauty.

What makes this final book in the trilogy so moving is that it is also a love story, a story of passion told in epistolary form, a tale of confronting and violating prevailing customs and norms about a "woman's place," a story of personal emancipation, and, perhaps more than anything else, a story of the love of and strength gained from family life. This is a book that should be read by all who are interested in how the intellectual migration helped shape modern America—one based on the pictures drawn by a remarkable woman nearing 100 years of age who experienced a wildly changing world.

—Jonathan R. Cole, John Mitchell Mason Professor of the University, Provost and Dean of Faculties (1989-2003), Columbia University

***

"Is there a way into the past to revive it not as memories but as a means to live more fully my present?" As we learn in the pages that follow, the event that prompts that initial question is the death of Ray Lorch, the brilliant mathematician with a passion for music who has been the author's beloved husband for almost forty years. "I still want to live—Ray tells his wife— but I am forced to live at another level from before and I have no control of it." When she desperately asks how she could help him, he responds, "You can only help me with your love...."

The Other Shore, the third volume that, after *Mamma and Her Village* and *Beyond Gibraltar,* completes Maristella de Panizza Lorch's trilogy, is a book about a geographical but also emotional and psychological journey. Maristella and Ray's eventual union led to the creation of a whole "new world" filled with projects, accomplishments (professional and personal), interests, books, adventures and friends. At the center of that microcosm, the love for their children raised between Riverside Drive in New York and the home nested in the Catskills where, as an ideal Ithaca, the family would always return. "Love", writes the author, "exists in what it creates." One of the most compelling gifts that one receives from this marvelous book is the idea that time is not just a meaningless succession of moments but a circular reality similar to the rings that mark the inner part of a growing tree: every line is enriched by its link and connection to the other. Ultimately, this highly poetic book is a celebration of the rooting power of memory and, with it, the belief that, more than any other force, Love is the true energy that, as Dante wrote in the *Divine Comedy*, "moves the sun and the other stars."

—Ingrid Rossellini, Ph.D., author of *Know Thyself: Western Identity from Classical Greece to the Renaissance*

***

In the final book of her trilogy, Medieval and Renaissance scholar Maristella Lorch has written a love story dedicated to her late husband, Edgar Raymond Lorch, the Swiss-American mathematician who, like her, also taught at Columbia University. But more than that, *The Other Shore* is the memoir of a woman who emigrates from Europe to America after World War II and persists in finding her place at a great American university of the '50s—a pioneering role model for women as she raises three daughters during a life filled with work, travel, and world figures.

Maristella sheds light on the internecine workings of a great American university, describing how she and the love of her life "dangerously sailed through two divorces, risking...at least my career at Barnard/Columbia." Throughout the book, Ray is the wise, enduring lone male surrounded by five interesting daughters—shades of Louisa May Alcott's *Little Women*. When one of their two own daughters, a journalist, takes off to Afghanistan, Pakistan, China and Africa, Ray reassures a worried Maristella: "That girl is made for open spaces."

Along the way, Maristella reflects on her near-century of living, meeting characters like the Afghan mujahed commander Abdul Haq, who has dinner at her Riverside, NY, home; Italy's three-time prime minister Giulio Andreotti, who supports her successful efforts to build Columbia University's Italian Academy for Advanced Studies in America on Amsterdam Avenue; and Polish opposition leader Lech Walesa. She takes the reader to Eastern Europe, on the cusp of the end of the Cold War; to the Italy of her birth and childhood; and to the land of the Masai of East Africa.

Maristella likens the journeys of her children and grandchildren across the modern-day world to the wandering knights of Medieval times, and she follows them wherever she can, even while looking back: "The spark to revive the past comes from the present. Only the past can shed new light on the present, enrich it with a new dimension we are slowly losing in today's world."

The Other Shore—a title that hints at both her life in the New World as well as her own approaching death—contains some flashbacks to the first two, *Mamma in Her Village* (2005) and *Beyond Gibraltar* (2013). Those books detail the historical hardships of her grandmother and mother, both widows, raising and educating children in the Austro-Italian Alps before, between, and during two World Wars. What unites the three books is Maristella's common theme of how love and strong traditions keep a family together over many generations.

—Pat Reber, formerly of AP and deutsche presse agentur (dpa)

***

When I was a freshman at Barnard I took a course called *Italian Literature in Translation* at the Casa Italiana. It was taught by Maristella de Panizza Lorch. I fell in love with Dante, Petrarca, and Italian literature in general. With all the enthusiasm of my young years, I promised myself that I would learn Italian so I could read Dante in the original.

My guide to Italian Literature was Professor Lorch. Looking back I wonder why it was so clear to me that I had to travel this road with her. I was not "*nel mezzo del cammin di nostra vita / mi ritrovai per una selva oscura / ché la diritta via era smarrita*" ("in the middle of the road of my life, I found myself in a dark wood in which the correct way was lost"). I was a recent graduate of the High School of Music and Art where I had studied painting, sculpture, silk screen printing and various academic subjects -- but my whole life I had loved poetry and written it, and now a new language, a new poetry was opened to me. I fell in love with Italian. I fell in love with the sound of the language, with its musicality, with its specificity—different from the specificity of American English.

I must also say that Professor Lorch was very different from all the other women who taught at Barnard and Columbia in those days. The year was 1959–60. Feminism was in retreat. The women who taught at Barnard were either lesbians with deep voices who did not acknowledge their sexuality or neurotic spinsters. You almost never met a woman who had children, who nursed them on campus, who spoke lovingly and happily of her home life and children and who was madly in love with her husband.

So Italian literature became bound up for me with the joy of being a woman and being an intellectual who knew that someday she wanted children.

Maristella was more rare on the Columbia campus than you can possibly imagine. She was a mother, a step-mother, a lover and an incredible scholar. Throughout my years at Barnard she remained a beacon in my life. Falling in love with Italian literature and language was part of falling in love with her.

Now, reading her book, *The Other Shore*, which deals with the end of her married life to Professor Ray Lorch—a mathematician and her soul mate—I am once again moved by what it means to be a great scholar, a great feminist and a great lover—things that often go together. I've always thought that women can do and be everything. I myself discovered that the birth of my daughter made me rather *more* than less creative. I come from a family of fierce feminist women but growing up in the fifties I was unsure about how I would combine all these things in my life.

Maristella gave me hope, and reading *The Other Shore* I now understand why. This is a beautiful book about a mature love affair that feeds both members of the couple and the children around them. Yet one of them has to depart this life before the other. As I discovered when I published *Fear of Dying*, most people don't want to think too much about their own mortality and yet it is only by embracing our mortality—the fear of it, the expression of it—that we come to understand who we really are. So Maristella has given me another gift.

How amazing is this book which tells the story of a man and woman who are equals and love each other completely and yet must lose each other at some point? What a gift. What a pleasure to read.

—Erica Jong, novelist, satirist, and poet, known particularly for her 1973 novel *Fear of Flying*

***

*to Ray
and to our families
of children and grandchildren
throughout the world*

*to Lavinia
who was with me
before she was born*

ACKNOWLEDGEMENTS

A book is never the work of a single person. I know I cannot recall all those who in some way shared my journey, but I trust they each know how our paths crossed. As the culmination of a trilogy almost half a century in the making, I owe a debt of gratitude to so many and to each person whose voice came alive in this book. These characters, collectively, form the soul of my story.

I can retrace the origins of our conversation about a trilogy to my Brazilian friend, Nelida Piñon, and to my Italian friends from the Valle d'Intelvi, Maria Corti and Annalisa Cima, as well as to my good friend from the University of Milan, Daniela Parisi and my Parisian friends and colleagues, Philippe and Geneviève Joutard. I recognize in this book the contribution of so many of my students over the past three quarters of a century, in particular of Ingrid Rossellini, most sensitive and intuitive interlocutor and listener, whom I have adopted as a daughter. I am thankful to all those who have enriched my life, both personal and academic—from the President of the Republic of Italy, Francesco Cossiga, to the Kenyan staff in Nairobi who welcomed me to their country and culture. I am grateful to the Italian Academy, its Director, David Freedberg, its staff and its Fellows, for having housed me in my corner office overlooking campus for the past twenty-seven years as I penned these three books, and to Rick Whitaker in particular for his filial devotion and affection. To my assistant Julie Ferrone I am forever grateful for the support in drafting the first version of this final volume.

Since leaving the physical space of the Academy, I have been assisted by an army of energetic young women and men with whom I explored the significance of the trilogy in my personal and professional life. Crystal Migwans enriched my writing with her interest in the narrative power of the physical object; Sandy Werb's bohemian and creative imagination kept me looking

21

beyond the here and now; Paola Omboni's affection and orderly approach to writing inspired me in moments where I might have given up; Mariagrazia DeLuca's spirit allowed me to explore the concept of blogging; Renata Bovaro's narrative gifts helped me stay focused; Cassandra Nwokah shared with me a lifelong love of the theatre, and my young Indian student, Shreyas Manohar, enriched my world with his kindness and respect. In these past months, a Colombian young man, Santiago Tobar Potes, a force of nature from the Columbia Undergraduate Scholars Program, has infused me with renewed enthusiasm, and my creative assistant and interlocutor, a writer in her own right, Stefania Calabrese, has been indispensable in allowing me to continue my work. This novel has been truly a work of intergenerational collaboration.

Throughout these past years, thanks to my daughters Lavinia and Donatella, I have been so fortunate as to have met regularly with my former Barnard student and oral historian, Lauren Taylor. Her wise and enriching probes into my life have helped me revisit moments of my past that were at times exhilarating and at times most painful. Lauren's interest in my century-long life has fueled my desire to believe that I still have something to share with humanity.

To Brian Smith I am so grateful not only for the care and attention with which he curated the photographs of my half century at the Casa Italiana and the Italian Academy but for his support in formatting this manuscript. In so many ways and over so many years, Brian has found his place as a family member amidst us.

I am grateful to each and every member of my family for having followed me and energized me on this long journey of the spirit in which the exploration of the past through the thick veils of memory proved as wondrous and illuminating as it could at times be tormenting. I thank my daughter Claudia for continuing to keep me abreast of life in today's Europe through her daily hour-long phone calls. I thank my son-in-law John for the patience with which he always listens to my stories when in Napanoch and for the special care which he always showed me when I was with him in Africa. I thank my son-in-law Michael, who included me from the start— forty years ago—in his and Lavinia's family, for the affectionate irony with which he teases and prods me along in my seemingly endless project, ferrying me every weekend to Napanoch and bringing me always back to the *hic et nunc*. I thank him in particular for having flown me in our long summers to log cabins in the wilderness of the American West and to islands in the blue during the darkest days of winter. Each of these adventures fed my imagination, but none as much as my experience of Barbuda.

I am grateful to all my grandchildren—Madeline, Nicholas, and Lucas, as well as to Celia and Charles, but to Alex in particular whose intellectual and emotional sensitivity always drew us together as interlocutors and companions in the story which is life. To Fiamma and Tristan I am forever grateful for their unswerving love not only for me but for the values that Napanoch and our family embodies. While Fiamma efficiently and sensitively tends to all my daily and practical needs as she prepares for her medical studies, Tristan, my "prince," is the patient and angelic companion with whom I rediscovered Italian neo-realistic film and the poetry of Yeats. Fiamma and Tristan are the family I have watched grow. It has kept me alive and given me purpose. Each one of my grandchildren, in different ways and from the balcony of different ages and different continents, expressed curiosity about my life in what increasingly appears to be another world. Their world is changing faster than mine ever did. I trust they will remember the value of their roots.

My daughter Ingrid read and reread this manuscript, sharing insights of both an ideological and structural nature. Ingrid is always anxious to start a new project and I am infinitely grateful to her for having been interested in looking over and commenting on my work over the years.

This book, final step of my journey, begins with Ray's and my love story on the gated campus of Columbia, and devolves into a wild exploration of the world and the people who inhabit it. I owe that adventure to my daughter Donatella who included me on her ventures, quests, and wanderings, allowing me to relive the adventures of my youth on new continents and by new rivers.

While Donatella allowed me the freedom to roam, my daughter Lavinia, to whom I dedicate this book, served as the anchor of my life and of my soul. She kept me going, physically and emotionally. She relentlessly encouraged me, critically reading, discussing, and editing my work for as long as I can remember. She is, as she always has been, my constant interlocutor, my co-author, my collaborator. Even in my darkest and weakest moments she always believed in me and fueled my desire to connect past and present, to weave the tapestry of our family with the silken threads of our unique experiences. When I met Ray I wanted Lavinia. Lavinia was with me before she was born.

Finally, this book is the product of my love for Ray and for the family we forged together in those years we were allowed to share on this earth, not only the genetic family but the intellectual and creative one that defies geography. I am grateful to all the living and the dead for having helped me reach this point.

Maristella de Panizza Lorch,

Napanoch, Memorial Day, 2018

"O frati", dissi, "che per cento milia
perigli siete giunti a l'occidente,
a questa tanto picciola vigilia

d'i nostri sensi ch'è del rimanente
non vogliate negar l'esperïenza,
di retro al sol, del mondo sanza gente.

Considerate la vostra semenza:
fatti non foste a viver come bruti,
ma per seguir virtute e canoscenza"

(Dante, *Inferno* XXVI. 112-120)

"'Brothers,'" I said, 'o you, who having crossed a
hundred thousand dangers, reach the west, to
this brief waking—time that still is left

unto your senses, you must not deny
experience of that which lies beyond
the sun, and of the world that is unpeopled.

Consider well the seed that gave you birth:
you were not made to live your lives as brutes,
but to be followers of worth and knowledge.'"

(Mandelbaum transl.)

Sì ch'io vedea di là da Gade il varco
folle d'Ulisse, e di qua presso il lito
nel qual si fece Europa dolce carco

(Dante, *Paradiso* XXVII. 82-84)

"So that, beyond Cadiz, I saw Ulysses'
mad course and, to the east, could almost see
that shoreline where Europa was sweet burden."

(Mandelbaum transl.)

26

When you are old and gray and full of sleep
And nodding by the fire, take down this book,
And slowly read, and dream of the soft look
Your eyes had once, and of their shadows deep;

How many loved your moments of glad grace,
And loved your beauty with love false or true;
But one man loved the pilgrim soul in you,
And loved the sorrows of your changing face.

And bending down beside the glowing bars,
Murmur, a little sadly, how love fled
And paced upon the mountains overhead,
And hid his face amid a crowd of stars.

William Butler Yeats

Our Ending

Everyone around me believes that everything has an end. But I alone have to cope with an end of You. And I refuse to accept it. I know now, five months after March 5, 1990, when you left me, that there must be the key to a new beginning somewhere in our past love story that stretches from 1951 to beyond 1990. I just do not know which way to follow, whether to reach up or down to grasp it…. How much does the past lean on my present? Is there a way into the past to revive it not as memories but as a means to live more fully my present? Is the revival of our love story a valid way to find the source of my own life as I lived it so far, a cup filled to the brim?

I leaf through our letters and poems of 1951-56, searching for the thread of Ariadne that might lead me out of the darkness of the labyrinth where I now live into the sun of once.

Dear Ray,

In December 1989, the month of my birthday and of Christmas, I realized I could only speak to you through the books I read to you at night, sitting near you on our blue love-seat while your three ancient clocks reminded us every hour on the hour that we were both still alive together…. You did not want to let go of our projects, not yet at least, but Life was receding from you one step at a time, a life you loved more than ever before, the Life you had so much loved with me day after day over forty years.

Now it's *Anna Karenina* that holds us together. What is there in this romantic Russian woman, I ask myself, that helps you hold on to life…. You follow her wanderings with your blue eyes wide open, holding my hand tight as she moves every night a bit closer to death—you so different from her, fearing for her… perhaps hoping for her, I don't know…. "She does not want to die. She wants to live…" you tell me, "she is down deep afraid of dying."

You are lost, I said to myself in January 1990. I had seen Christmas, New Year's, and before then Lavinia's or Vinnie's and Michael's Ph.D. defenses in November 1989, which we had been so fervently waiting for. I had seen them all through a microscope, searching for the old you, at times almost convinced I could find you... I kept on saying to myself out loud that until we knew the answers to your latest tests—that is, before discovering the cause of the obstruction that destroyed your body—we should live in Limbo, as if Hell did not exist a few steps away from those dignified pagan philosophers you used to admire when you first sat in my Dante classes.... Work helped me a bit, my obsession with deadlines, as if your life depended on my sending off on time the proofs of a book or of an essay or obtaining an improbable approval for a Columbia proposal from a precarious Italian government.

Then came the by-now usual visits to the doctors. First to Tom Jacobs, as wise as he is knowledgeable. Pressed by my questions, he said he was not God, but looking at his face, I read in dark letters that you were the victim of an unconquerable illness. Dr. Weber gave me a final blow in shining words. Cancer. Three to Six months. Dr. Ford offered a beam of light— perhaps you could be operated?—in the darkness in which I was plunged. I wished I could hang on to that light, speak to somebody who could hope with me against all hope for a while longer, but Vinnie, who has always been my constant support, was away. There was nobody I could turn to but you. You and me. Alone in darkness. You who had given me the light of life. You needing me desperately and I was incapable of helping you. That was yesterday... Today I know I must give you up and Time is running short for me to pour on you all of my love.

I know I am wasting time.... It took me too long to accept my new sleeping quarters away from you. The first night I got to the floor of the living room, on cushions removed from the sofas, I was angry and resentful. Then I was infinitely lonely. At Christmas, after the household had quieted down, I finally fell on those cushions as the place where I could recover my energy, and I slept. The living room, besides our bedroom—I thought—

is the corner of the apartment we furnished with greater care and love through forty years, every piece of furniture telling, through its shape, a human story within a wide-open space, without doors, overlooking the River we both love…. That is what I tell myself as I lie at the feet of your antique desk, surrounded by your clocks….

You never told me why you collected antique clocks. As they surround me now every night, three of them ringing Time century after century, they fascinate me. When the thought of you wakes me up during the night I rejoice at their music as a guarantee of your voice forever. Yet, last night I had to silence one of them…. It was hard, like silencing the song of your voice within me…. The cause of my crime was your desk…. Yesterday, before Vinnie, you, and I left for the hospital, the most used drawer of your father's antique desk could not be opened. Michael worked on it for hours while we were away. In order to open it he had to cut it in the back. It was an operation he carried out delicately, as the son of an eye surgeon, delivering to me afterwards the tiny eighteenth-century nails for you to keep.

I have them here with me now. In the banging and shaking desk however, your father's German clock began ringing again —after a long silence. You warned me about it last night. "It rings again," you said, "but softly, every hour on the hour." During the night, however, that venerable clock rang not softly like the other two but harsh and loud, and not every hour either but every quarter of an hour. Until four o'clock I listened to it patiently, then almost unconsciously I bolted up and in the dim light of the night groped for it among the unopened letters piled on your desk and raised it in my arms. While I carried it it rang so softly, gently, melodiously that it broke my heart. Crying, I brought it to the kitchen and placed it as far away as I could from the living room, over the washing machine. Then I grabbed a blanket and suffocated the clock under it. When I had returned to my cushions on the floor, I could not sleep because I was unconsciously listening to it. The clock was silent. Finally, exhausted, I cried myself to sleep.

"The piano is ready for you to play," the piano tuner had said last night. You had replied a hurried 'thank you' and closed the door behind him. Having made the effort of writing a check and exchanging a few words you had no more strength left and you fell back on the sofa, without touching the piano you had been longing to play. During the night, however, after moving the clock, I could have sworn that I distinctly heard the Chopin pieces you played for me throughout the years, from the moment I first visited you in your old home on Amsterdam Avenue in the Fall of 1951. As unmusical as I am, I could recognize your Chopin among the thunderclaps of a storm. I woke up alone and, in order to dispel the clouds of my dream, I walked on tiptoes along the hall of books to Dony's room, tempted to slide into her bed to warm myself near her, but looking at her peacefully sleeping, I didn't dare to disturb her... As I winded my way back along the long hall, I looked into our bedroom....

Lying quietly in our small eighteenth-century Dutch marquetry bed, you had only enough oil in your lamp to keep yourself alive.

Back in the living room, I decided to put your desk in order. I made neat packages of the letters and returned the German clock to its home where it rings while I write this letter.

It is 8 am now. Dony is in the kitchen reading the paper. I prepared everything for her breakfast. She will probably stop by and give me her cursory kiss before leaving for the New York Times. Or perhaps not. I take her as she is, generous at heart. Lucy sleeps soundly after her last cancer radiation in order to regain her strength and go to Italy to visit her sister and her nephew Ninetto, the only family that truly loves her. Or so she says—an hour later she calls it an illusion. She lives with illusions. I love her because she is so good to you. With me she is now as bossy as a woman could be to another woman who does not put up any resistance. I never met anybody like her who has an easy solution for every problem. Even for her illnesses.

You slept peacefully last night. When I came by your room you told me so. Monday or Tuesday we'll hear the "news" from the doctors, either the beginning of a new fight or a most painful adaptation to the old. I refuse to think about it. All I know is that I must do something *real* to show you my *love*. I must prove to you that you helped me to be what I am today, you the only person in the whole world to whom I can open my heart. That's why this letter is much longer than I envisaged. As I write I live with the illusion that you are near me...listening to me as usual.

Again and again I ask myself why I suggested *Anna Karenina* for our nightly semi-mystical encounters, a novel that had shocked me as an adolescent when we lived as guests of the Russian colony of "Villa Moskau." I later analyzed the novel for "Romantic Agony," a course Barry Ulanov and I invented at Barnard in the early fifties—you might remember. That was precisely the period when you and I had just met and were searching for ways to reach each other with hundreds of notes and letters in order to make sense of what was happening to us —we had a love of life and a fear of, or rather disgust for, a hypocritical society.... Tolstoy's novel describes in fascinating terms a world of conflicting emotions surfacing through thoughts and visions, an intricate web of forces which is life as we lived it from that December in 1952 to our meeting in Genova in the summer of 1954 when we suddenly decided to join forces in facing the future no matter what and build a life together...

Today, when I look back at that period, "Genova" which called for us to divorce—a word unknown in my world so far— seems to me to have happened by chance. Anna Karenina instead is not given a chance, you tell me. Tolstoy's story allows us to live our own decision in all of its complexity. It allows us to see our world at a distance as we face death together, purified suddenly of all the heavy burden that drew Anna to suicide.

"Ray, you are moving into a dark tunnel," I told you last night. "I cannot follow you anymore...."

"No," you answered softly, "I am moving into a sunset...the lights are dying out."

"The lights of *Life*?" I asked terrified.

"I still want to live, but I am forced to live at another level from before and I have no control over it...." "I wish I could help you."

"You can only help me with your love.... But please don't force yourself. Be who you are.... You have the most sweet and generous personality...but you are a force of nature. You are for me Life itself.... I was lucky to meet you and have your love. Thank you for it...."

Our love of once feeds the world of today as together we face your death. It is like the love of once, yet it is different. Life itself changes around us. As our body decays, the essence of Life within it envisages the faint shadows of another shore. As one of the two lovers prepares to leave before the other, he instinctively longs to be remembered. Yet for the survivor love that conquers time is not made of memories. In its very roots, love finds the reasons for what it is beyond the Time of the clocks—so different near the end of the road and yet so much the same as when it was born. Memories reinforce love when it still exists. They cannot revive it. Love exists in what it creates.

All I can pledge to you, my dear Ray, as you are about to vanish from the royal park of Riverside like Eurydice in the sweet twilight of a sunset, is that I will try to retrace before I die the voyage of our life together in its key moments. I shall try to relive it in order to better understand why you, today, in your frightening weakness, physically deprived of almost everything that makes for Life, still are and shall continue to be the source of strength in my life, everything that I most treasure, the only person I can turn to when the world around me darkens and I desperately need somebody to whom I can speak.

Based in part on the hundreds of letters we exchanged from 1952 to 1955 and then from 1986 to yesterday, our new voyage will be inspired by what unites us today: a life I shall continue to live with all the strength of which I am capable within our family and into the wide world.

The Great War and the decision to cross the Ocean years before I met you were only early episodes in my life, a life I shall continue to live as a precious gift, fully, completely, to the marrow, filling my cup to the brim. That is what you taught me, inspired, I surmise, by that vision of mathematical infinity with which I had blindly fallen in love, long before I met you, as an adolescent lost on a glacier in the heart of my homeland. Thank you, Ray, your M.

***

Ray never read my letter. He was depressed when I wrote it and I did not have the courage to read it aloud to him, though so much of what I wrote was subject of our conversations.... I read to him instead a letter my daughter Claudia had sent to both of us from her home in Paris. After several attempts to leave her, her husband had finally abandoned the family once and for all shortly after she had returned to Paris with her children from a visit to our refuge in the Catskills.

Paris, February 1, 1990

Dearest Mamma and Poppy,

I am writing to both of you because I want you to know how much I treasure you both in my heart as one entity. Not two but one in love, understanding, and serenity in a very trying moment of your lives.

As paradoxical as it may seem to you at this time, I truly envy you for your tenacity, tolerance, and faith in each other through the years which allow you to live this difficult moment as what seems to me like a beautiful sunset. I speak of sunset because dusk, not dawn, is for me the most glorious moment of the day, when the sun gives nature its richest colors. At dawn all remains to be done. Dusk gives us the gift of a day well spent.

You are among those lucky few whom many may envy for having reaped together the most wonderful sunset. You are for us, your girls, not merely examples but ideals hard to follow because you gave so much of yourselves not only to each other but to all who surrounded you, and above all to us, your girls....

Perfection is an endless quest and I don't think of you as perfect. Poppy's annoying trait was always his 'sarcasm,' or 'skepticism.' Mommy's was her hyperactivity. Though very close to us especially in our studies, she was always deeply involved in something of her own which she enjoyed and to which she gave all of herself. In these last years, Poppy, you have replaced 'sarcasm' with a gentle irony that better fits your nature and allows you to take the world as it is.... As for Mommy's involvement, most of the time it turns into constructive energy with astonishing results. We did at times misunderstand both of you (as you misunderstood us), but the charm, love, and warmth among us was never broken. We had with you the best fun a child could have in life....

I should call this charm 'the family,' because your greatest achievement was 'the family.' You gave to us girls this magnificent 'refuge' within which and from which to create. You should be proud of it in times of success as in times of family hardship as we all go through now.... while Europe celebrates what you both longed for, its unification....

It is no doubt because of how your raised us—within a strong, loving and happy family—that I am now struggling so hard to maintain the family I worked so hard to build.

Thank you both for being what you are and for having given me all you did. I want you to know that in this difficult moment for all of us you are both present in my prayers. We learned from you how to fight and to pray together. Love, Claudia.

Ray dictated to me his answer to Claudia's letter shortly after we received it. Claudia's letter had energized him, he said.

My dear Claudia,

Thank you for thinking of us together as a unity and for praying for us. We need prayers. We spent a week of anxiety about the biopsy. We don't know what goes on among the doctors privately. Here is what they tell us. Ford excludes colon cancer but agrees with the others that it is some sort of cancer. Jacobs calls it 'undifferentiated fast-growing cells" treatable with some kind of chemotherapy. "I am not God, he says, just a doctor...." Ingrid and Lucia were with Mommy when she got the call. I am told Lucy kept on making the pasta and Ingrid said it was too much for her and refused to comment....

Dony made the front page of the NYT again with a murderer in the Bronx caught after 43 years. Poor guy... I pity him and so, I think, does Dony, though she pretends to be professionally objective.... Vinnie revives me as usual as she takes care of me while fervently praying with Mommy for the treatable cancer. We must fight back, Mommy and Lavinia say.... So, I fight back.

My love,

Ray

***

May 5, 1990

Ray died on March 5 at 3:10 pm in one of the armchairs of our lobby at 445 Riverside. He had come from the hospital where, with Lavinia and Michael, he had been waiting two hours for the result of his latest biopsy. Inconclusive as usual. As Lavinia held his hand, he closed his eyes and she felt his spirit flee from his tortured flesh.

Ray never mentioned death. Like his father he believed in life. So that morning he had sent me downtown for an important appointment instead of allowing me to go to the doctor with him. Lavinia and Michael would be with him to hear the predictably inconclusive result of his latest biopsy.

The night before, at 1 a.m., I had finished reading to him *Anna Karenina*. He listened with his eyes closed as usual. At the end, he thanked me in a feeble voice and kissed me on the forehead. "You gave the greatest gift of my life. I wish I had enough strength to tell you." I knew he did not want us to end with

Anna's suicide. Ray didn't have to tell me. I wish he could have played Chopin once more for me.

He greeted me at the door the next morning from his usual position on the living room loveseat with a faint smile: "You are beautiful, and I love you." I said, "Say it louder." With an effort, smiling ironically, he repeated "I love you. And now go." These were his last words to me. He didn't allow me to see him dying.

He lived at home like a king surrounded by his seven women. I was in the past years his connection with the world outside the home. He worked for forty years to make me what I am, that is the good and useful part of me. As for the bad part he never rejected it. For forty years he loved me as I am: he knew we cannot live by reason alone. He used to say, "You are my masterpiece."

Michael carried his body to a police car that appeared on the Drive before the ambulance we had called. He was declared dead at Saint Luke's hospital. Dony, summoned by the New York Times from her Police Beat in the Bronx, arrived in time to see her father before his body was taken to the morgue. She gave me his watch and took for herself his wedding ring, which is now on the finger of her husband, Johannes Zutt. A week later she gave me in lieu of Ray's ring an antique gold circle I still wear around my neck alongside Ray's "Phi Beta Kappa" key on an antique gold watch chain Ray had given me on our wedding day.

Ray was buried on Saturday in our little Civil War cemetery in a woody grove in the Catskills, close to the place we call home. The delay gave Michael time to look for the kind of coffin that would please his mentor in mathematics and in the art of living. He finally found a handmade bier in a Jewish Orthodox community carved out of a single oak trunk, kept together without a single iron nail. Since the Catholic church in Ellenville refused to receive the body of a Protestant for the rite of Christian burial, Ray was honored with a serene Mass at the Lutheran Church. This would have pleased his deceased parents, a British Episcopalian and a Swiss French Calvinist, descendant of the

French poet Racine. The first crocuses pierced the ground around us as the earth received his body.

Among the colleagues, philosophers, writers, political men besides mathematicians, scientists and people from all walks of life who wrote in reaction to our announcement of Ray's death, the closest friend of the family, the philosopher Ernesto Grassi, plunged me into the void I was desperately trying to avoid. He was so overwhelmed by Ray's serene 'sunset' and so envious of him as to beg Lavinia and me to go to see him immediately. Older than Ray and quite ill, he felt his time had come to join Ray.... What Ernesto needed was Ray himself with his half serious, half ironic way of speaking that he so admired. Ernesto died a year after Ray. I never found the strength to go to see him.

After thirty-eight years of life with Ray, I am now learning to rediscover time. Our love within time. I tremble in reliving the intensity with which I searched for Ray in 1953 and Ray for me in 1986. When I had Ray and could see and touch and hear him, patience was not one of my virtues. I always wanted more of him. Now I am slowly learning how to live with his new intangible presence. I learn, and then I forget. I can hold on to his soul through words alone.

"Nec enim parvus aut index animi sermo est aut sermonis moderator est animus. Alter pendet ex altero" (Petrarch. De Rebus Familiaribus. Ep. VIII]. (For the word is not a small indicator of the soul nor is the soul the master of the word. One depends upon the other.)

Our Beginning

October 15, 1951 was one of those crystal-clear early Fall days in which the Barnard/Columbia campus looked like the earthly paradise of upper Manhattan. Not the slightest breeze touched the still green trees, giving the impression of an eternal summer. The Hudson flowed lazily towards the bay beyond the green curtain of Riverside Park. Classes were about to start, and students lingered on the benches of the Barnard "Jungle," a tree-shaded enclave looking over the tennis court between the two buildings that constituted the "College"—Milbank and Barnard Hall. Students, neatly dressed and nicely combed, were busying themselves, within the "Jungle," with peaceful activities such as discussing courses, books in hand. To my relief, as far as I could see, the second World War had come and gone without leaving any particular imprint on the behavioral pattern of this great American campus.

At age 31, having crowned four years of fighting for survival in the War in Europe with four awesome years of fighting for survival in New York, I was now delighted to slide into the mysteries of this beautifully mysterious American acropolis. I had just been hired as an assistant professor by Barnard College. On that peaceful October afternoon, waiting for classes to start, I sensually savored the idea that I had finally arrived where I had originally intended to arrive, within the vast continent that lay open to me when I walked off the "General Muir" in February 1948. I cherished with deep pleasure the idea of myself, an unknown and insignificant war-bride from overseas dispensing knowledge to America from the Columbia campus. Oblivious of all responsibilities that my new life entailed, I was also relaxing into the feeling that, after three years of five-hour-a-day commuting to a College lost in the green pastures of New Jersey, I was finally stationed on the blessed island of Manhattan, in the heart of New York.

True, I had in appearance regressed from the impressive title of "Associate Professor of German, French, and Italian" that I had enjoyed in New Jersey to the plain "Assistant Professor of Italian." Yet, for some reason I only heard the sound of "Assistant Professor at Barnard College, comma, Columbia University" as it rang in my ears like the bells of St. Peter's Basilica when on Easter morning they fill the Roman sky with their triumphant hymn to Christ's resurrection. And so I repeated those magic words again and again to myself as I sat in my new office in the basement of Milbank Hall, on the extreme Northwest corner of the building: "Assistant Professor of Italian at Barnard College, comma, Columbia University." And as the words flowed from my mouth, I allowed myself to bask in their warm echo to my heart's content.

In my state of innocent bliss, however, I was not completely unaware that snakes might be lurking in the high luxurious grass and that because of my ignorance I was vulnerable to blows from an environment unknown to me. My predecessor in that office, I was told, was an old spinster who considered as her property everything Italian on the Columbia campus West of Broadway and had thus strenuously fought against the infiltration of any 'Italian' hailing from the East. I vaguely sensed some danger was lurking somewhere, but for the time being I preferred to ignore it. There were other issues to worry about. When the Dean of the Faculty had introduced me to that office as my 'kingdom,' I had to plow my way into it, so clogged was the room with books, copy books, bluebooks, records, old pictures, bric a brac of all sort. The spinster, I was told, had died suddenly during her sabbatical year in her beloved Italy, land of her ancestors, which she was visiting in order to collect memorabilia of the War that had just swept through the peninsula. *Mors tua vita mea*, I thought, my heart overflowing with gratitude for that unknown benefactor. I imagined that wherever she was on the other side of Gibraltar perhaps she was satisfied that I, a shipwreck of that horrible War, having crossed Gibraltar on my own, now sat comfortably among the memorabilia she had collected.

"What do you ask for a salary?" the Chairman of the five-member committee who interviewed me in early June 1951 had asked me. "The salary is of no importance," I had answered proudly. Of course, I could have explained in detail why I didn't care. If I have to live in America, I could have said, it can only be in Manhattan. I fought to get here through four hard years. But now I am tired of commuting while caring for a small child at home, a husband studying without much success, a war hero brother-in-law and a beloved sister fighting to legitimize their presence in the US.... I could have explained further: "I love this campus. It is my home in America by the will of God." This I could have said and much more. But I didn't.

The telephone cut my daydreams short. My very own telephone on my very own desk! It was Maria Melano, the gentle Public Relations Officer of Barnard, wife of the Italian Consul of Newark, New Jersey, offering me a tour of the College premises. I was delighted.

Among the most astonishing treasures of Barnard was its Library. With the help of my hostess, I had borrowed there an armful of books, when on our way out I noticed a gentleman walking towards us from the end of the long hall. He was tall and blond and held a book open in his hands which he promptly closed as he reached us, as if he had planned to meet with us.

To my surprise, the gentleman who introduced himself to me as some kind of professor, was not a common American professor according to my four years of American experience. He acted like a man of the world, spoke fluent French with a Swiss accent, joked lightly about everything I had so far considered holy—in sum, he dealt with me and my friend as if we were society ladies in a Roman salon rather than workers in an American Women's College. Jokingly he also said he would soon learn Italian now that the College had acquired the services of a charming lady like me....

I was appalled by the encounter simply because it did not fit into what I had imagined life at Barnard College. Perhaps he was trying to impress me, I told Mrs. Melano after he finally left. No, said my host, he was trying to be kind to me. Americans were slowly beginning to take an interest in Italy, that is in spite of the war... I should be happy and grateful...What did she mean, I asked, vaguely perturbed in my present state of bliss. The war had cast a black shadow on Italy, she added with a mysterious expression, as if a cloud had suddenly obscured the sun. Was teaching Italian on the Columbia campus a kind of diplomatic mission? I thought to myself. Was I here to mend the wounds inflicted by a war?

Attracted as I was, however, by the marvels of my new kingdom, I soon forgot about the Gentleman Professor and the problems he was to pose. But a few weeks later, it might have been a month, the tall blond Professor took a seat near me at a faculty meeting and, showing little interest for what was going on at the meeting, engaged with me in a lively *sotto-voce* French on futilities such as the color of my dress and the beauty of my pearls.... Faculty meetings in 1951 took place in what was then the chemistry lab of the College, in Milbank Hall, where now, in the renovated building, is the stately Spanish Room. We sat on uncomfortably high stools. I was wearing—he told me months later—a purple knitted two-piece woolen dress that fitted me perfectly. After the meeting was over, he followed me to my office, made himself comfortable in the old armchair and, to my surprise, ironically commented on the fatal operation my predecessor underwent in Italy: "Gossip has it that the Italian surgeon did his best," he said, "to find the tumor, but...Madame was such a compact ball of fat that he didn't succeed." After some meandering in elegant conversation in his slightly accented *genevois* French, the worldly Professor bluntly asked me to admit him to my course in elementary Italian. I startled, blushed and asked him for his name. I had difficulty, I said, remembering Anglo-Saxon names. He spelled it for me: *Edgar Raymond Lorch.* We smiled at each other with embarrassment. I got up and promised I would think about it. As soon as he left the office, I rushed to the Barnard Bulletin. There he was! The Chairman of the Mathematics Department! How dare he look into my business? I was appalled. A Full Professor with tenure taking advantage of a newly arrived Assistant Professor! I was fuming. Barnard College had accepted my candidacy. I was the last person interviewed from approximately seventy well qualified individuals, a true triumph for a European whom America had condemned so far to commuting. No sooner was I introduced to the forbidden garden that a spy had descended upon me to evaluate my performance.... I took a deep breath and decided on a strategy for my legitimate defense. I had known worse situations than the present one.

When two days later Professor Lorch, Chairman of the Department of Mathematics, appeared in my office, I received him with much greater kindness than he had expected (he later confessed). Of course, I remembered Mrs. Melano's words! If he wanted to learn Italian in a hurry—since he was to appear at the University of Rome as the first Fulbright Lecturer in Mathematics in the fall of 1952—I was offering him private tutoring in my own office. No need for him to appear in a classroom. To my surprise the Professor looked at me in dismay. No, he had no intention of taking advantage of me in any way, he said. Now what was he thinking, I wondered. That I was offering him something other than Italian lessons? ... Always speaking in French, I resorted then to another stratagem: since he knew French, Spanish, German, and Latin he was most certainly over-qualified for elementary Italian. I could admit him, however, to my Intermediate Italian. He accepted reluctantly.

I felt sure that, given the short time span, he could never catch up on an entire year of material. He could choose between being humiliated or simply renouncing his scheme. A few days later Professor Lorch nervously entered his first class in Intermediate Italian. He had received from me all the books ahead of time and had prepared his lesson: there was one weekly session of composition, one on Dante, one on Manzoni or D'Annunzio. He sat near a girl, Frieda Kisch, with wide blue eyes, a thick *chevelure* of dark hair and big breasts. She was fast and gifted. He soon began writing notes to her. They laughed together and their behavior bothered me. How could eminent American professors allow themselves to behave this way in front of colleagues? Were they making fun of my teaching? But within weeks the professor turned out to be exceptionally good. He fenced through grammar and syntax like a musketeer, winning all tournaments and he soon began reciting aloud Dante or *La figlia di Jorio*. The whole class swam with delight into the Paolo and Francesca episode. Perhaps the girls saw our blond mathematician as a sort of Paolo. Some of them, I am sure, would have liked to be his Francesca...or thought that I would be the fortunate one to play that role. They all laughed peevishly when he cracked a joke. He enjoyed the class, he told me, more than he had expected.

One day in late November he did not show up for class. The next day I found a note in my mailbox: "Cara Professora...", he apologized in Italian for the absence. He had to attend a committee meeting. I corrected the errors in red and blue pencil and sent the note back to him. He gratefully acknowledged my corrections. Committees seemed to increase as the season progressed towards December. Every time the professor had to attend one he wrote a note... until the time came when he wrote a note for no reason whatsoever. I brought those notes home and showed them to my sister Bona. The professor wrote a few lines using charming Italian expressions of naive admiration for his superb teacher in small, perfectly round calligraphy. At times he produced a linguistic pun. It was up to Bona and me to decipher it.

My household at Bennett Avenue was a happy one in spite of our many worries: my brother-in-law, Eddie, had been very ill and both he and my sister were groping in the dark for a visa; little four-year-old Claudia had begun attending the Columbia kindergarten called "Greenhouse" because it was housed in a real greenhouse. In the morning she was in the hands of a bi-racial middle-aged lady called Mrs. McMullen who considered little Claudia a goddess with a mind of her own. The afternoon she spent with me on campus. At night she came home a true hellion who fell asleep exhausted while she ate dinner.

My husband Claude, the veteran of four landings whose great moment had been during the war in Europe, should have never listened to my advice about leaving the army. After he lost his first civilian job in New York, he wandered around the apartment for three years with the illusion that by taking courses at Columbia he could perhaps someday get a degree. After all, he was a Harvard alumnus. I had given up hope on that degree before I got my new job at Barnard. At the same time, I had overcome the bitterness and resentment I had felt towards him during my pregnancy and after Claudia's birth because of how he coped lightheartedly with the most elementary necessities of life. Leaving me to fight alone proved, he was convinced, that in the end I would win.

I had learned to take Claude as an essential part of my American environment, a proof that each of us has to figure out life on his own. I did not realize, during that golden autumn of 1951, that my attitude towards Claude was the prelude of an emotional independence destined to become the equivalent of emotional indifference. As soon as I had set foot on solid ground and safely landed, that is established my emotional independence, I could easily do without him. My family was Claudia and my sister. I was thankful to Claude for having helped me to call Bona and Eddie to America six months after my arrival. He could be thankful to me on many accounts. We were even, I thought in my frequent moments of disillusionment.

Despite very hard times and little money, Bona and I at Bennett Avenue enjoyed moments of laughter when we could make fun of the world around us and of ourselves in spite of our misery. We had overcome together the unbearable nostalgia of the only true family we had known in our life—our mother, brother, and sister whom we had left behind in Rome.

Professor Lorch and his notes became part of my nightly after dinner conversations and amusement with Bona. "Who is he?" she would ask. "Describe him to me." Sitting alone at the kitchen table, everybody asleep around us, Bona and I, upon careful analysis of the document, agreed that the handsome mathematician was a born linguist who had decided to cleverly manipulate a language totally new to him for his own purpose. What was the purpose of his notes? A showoff of bravura? A joke Columbia style? I should be careful, Bona kept on repeating. I had been dreaming too much about "Columbia." It was time for me to face the place as a reality and behave accordingly.

Bona was right. I was well aware by now that Columbia had been for me not a reality, but the object of my dreams, since the very first day of my arrival in New York. The day after our arrival, on March 17, 1947, I had walked with Claude from Grand Central Station to Washington Heights, with the intention of delivering a letter by my Roman Professor to the then President of Columbia, Nicholas Murray Butler, unaware that he was no longer President and that Columbia was an awesome institution. Failing in our mission, Claude and I had fallen asleep out of exhaustion on campus, at the feet of the Alma

Mater. After Claude and I subsequently also failed miserably at presenting our *Millionaire Naples*, Claude's translation of a brilliant Italian play, I had mostly lost contact with Barnard and Columbia, though Professor Hadas of the Classics Department, had employed me to tape Greek plays in the original Greek, and this provided me with enough money for a brief visit to Rome. In time, three out of four members of my American family had also registered as graduate students at Columbia. I had soon fallen off the list out of exhaustion and lack of money to pay tuition but had finally made it three years later to enter the magic kingdom as a member of the Faculty at Barnard....

"This is a case of courtship! You must watch out!" Bona declared finally "A courtship American or rather Columbia style.... Try to remember another case of American courtship. Claude's, for instance."

"Claude was not a Professor..." I replied.

"Professor or not... Columbian or not. This note reveals a human being... a male human being who wants to get close to you.... You must watch out!"

She stopped and looked inquisitively at me. "Perhaps the Professor was encouraged by your own behavior towards him."

She grabbed a folder with my class material and rapidly went through it. "Here is a letter of yours!" she said triumphantly:

"Dear Professor, I did not send you back your last letter as usual, with the due corrections. There are cases in which corrections seem out of place. Your Italian was enchanting, errors and all."

I had then delved into esoterical deliberations on the use of a foreign language by cultured adults. While I had thanked him for the kind words he had for me, I had dared to venture, according to Bona, on dangerous grounds: "I don't find it too difficult to stop acting as a *maestra* because I feel you can be in more than one sense a Maestro to me..."

"Here you are!" Bona commented with the firm tone of voice that came natural to her when she thought she grasped a truth ignored by her interlocutor. "It was you who used first the pun *'Maestro'* versus *'Maestra'*. Although the note is framed by a 'Dear Professor' at the opening and by the official formula in the end: 'To you, dear Professor, the expression of my most cordial friendship,' it is crystal clear to me that you opened the door to the wolf. You shouldn't be surprised now that the wolf, like in the fable, entered the house...".

Caught in a Net

Bona was right. In the notes that followed the wolf indeed took full possession of the house he had entered with my tacit consent. On December 4, addressing me with *"Molto cara Amica"* ("very dear friend"), the Professor professes deep tenderness with the utmost respect. On December 6, in a note that daringly opens with "Maristella!", he declares gratitude for my friendship towards his wife. He also hints to an important event that had taken place the evening before in his apartment: the exchange of a "furtivo bacio" or furtive kiss, and my addressing him for the first time as "Ray."

"Grazie a Lei, Maristella." The letter concludes. *"Un giorno dirò 'grazie a te.'"* ("One day I shall thank you with [the familiar] 'tu'.")

Neither Bona nor I had cared whether he was married or not, until one day I found out by chance. I had met him at the exit of Milbank Hall just before Thanksgiving. Walking towards the "Jungle" he had asked me if I was married. I had reversed the question. "Yes," he answered, "I am married and have three children." A few days later he asked me to meet his wife. She had developed a great admiration for me, he said. Soon after, Else, his wife, was sitting in my Elementary Italian. A Norwegian who spoke French well, she was able to learn Italian faster than the rest of the class.

After class, Else would come to my office. Soon thereafter, as her confidante, I entered a new strange realm of human relationships which taught me more about life than anything I had lived through before. Her desperate fight for emotional survival, torn as she had been for many years between her lover and her family were for me scattered leaves of a fascinating novel without any plausible solution in sight.

Else had been for weeks my student in "Elementary Italian," when on December 7, 1951, I was invited to dinner by my two special students, the Professor and his wife, who vied for my attention out of gratitude for the pleasure of attending my courses. Who would have ever thought that 'Italian,' the subject I had despised as a classicist upon my arrival in America and that rated the lowest on the MLA scale at the time, could produce such miracles—an invitation to dinner by an eminent colleague and his wife—, I thought to myself as I rode the elevator to the Lorchs' apartment on the last floor of 121st Street and Amsterdam Avenue.

I was met at the door by the children, eight-year-old Duncan and the six-year-old twins, Ingrid and Madeleine, thin tall girls with blond braids, all three curious to see what I looked like. Ray and Else led me in a festive mood to their living room softly lit by a floor lamp, the piano on one side of the long sofa.

The Lorchs' favorite drinks were port and vermouth. That evening it was vermouth. I sat, surrounded by the admiring family for quite a while, sipping Italian vermouth, answering questions about my family, my home, the War, my arrival in America, Claude and little Claudia, my sister Bona and her unfortunate war hero Eddie who was striving hard to secure a legitimate place in the American sun.... I didn't dare ask any questions of my hosts. I gathered they were Euro-Americans, she a Norwegian, he British and French/Swiss. The children spoke French at home. His maternal language was French. She adored French.

After the children had disappeared in their rooms, I moved with Else to the kitchen. Ray followed us, glass in hand. The first physical contact between the Professor and me took place while Ray and I walked back from the kitchen to the living room. The hall was long, narrow, shelves of books on one side, pictures on the other. Very dimly lit, it smelled of the food being cooked in the kitchen and echoed with the noise of children playing behind closed doors. I was carrying a vase I had just filled with a bunch of violets I had brought as a gift to the family. Ray was walking behind me. Suddenly, for no special reason, I felt his presence so close to me it made me dizzy. I stopped without turning. He bent slightly down towards me, and I felt his breath gently caressing my neck. Then his lips grazed my skin like a slight breeze. I walked on without turning. The hall seemed interminable. When we finally reached the living-room he took the vase from me and placed it on the table, holding my hands in his. Instinctively, I kissed his hand. Then he sat at the piano. Chopin filled the room.

"Grazie, Ray" I said when he was finished.

My instinctive reaction to Ray's kiss was documented in a poem in uncouth German that I had scribbled on a piece of paper ripped out of an agenda late that spring. I was perhaps trying to continue in the playful tone Ray had started with his first 'note,' although by now the early playful notes had been replaced by love letters, at times anguishing documents of the painful situation in which I found myself.

My German poem, a fun legitimization of the sweet deception of a lover's kiss, reflects a playful moment in an otherwise dramatic love story. Ray preserved that poem with a date:

Ein Küss macht Frühling

Hast mich geküsst im Winter...
...Ich wusste schon
dass ich es gleich
vergessen sollte...
Und doch dein Kuss
gab solche Wonne
ich hab dich gleich geliebt

...

Und doch dein Kuss gab solche
Lust wie konnte ich es vergessen?

...

Und wieder ist ein Frühling da
mit Knospen und mit Trieben
und wieder ist die Erde voll
von Pärchen die sich lieben.
So geht es nun schon manches Jahr
und immer hört sie gern
was ihr Geliebter zärtlich lügt
beim Glanz der frommen Sternen.

...

Wie dumm wär es sonst das Menschenleben.
Wahr ist das Tier. Der Mensch allein kann
sich zum Schein erheben.

A Kiss Makes Spring

You kissed me in winter...
I already knew
I should have
Forgotten it immediately...
And yet your kiss
Gave such delight
I loved you instantly

...

And yet your kiss gave such desire
How could I forget it?

...

And again spring has come
With buds and sprouts
And again the earth is full
With couples in love.
So it goes many a year
And she always likes to hear
The tender lies of her lover

Shining in the pious stars.
...
How dull would human life otherwise be.
Genuine is the animal. Only man
Can soar in sham.
(trans. Justin Snider)

That *furtivo bacio*, that furtive kiss, as light as a feather's caress, opened up a new world to us. The day after the kiss, it was December 8, my birthday. Ray showed up towards evening in my office with twelve carnations in hand. We left the office together and sat on a bench of Riverside Drive. The story he told me then introduced me into a world I would have never imagined could exist within Columbia. It shocked and disoriented me. It changed not only my 'dream' of Columbia but my whole life.

Ray began the conversation by reminding me that my birthday coincided with the day after the anniversary of Pearl Harbor and asked me what my reaction to it had been when it happened.

"I wish I had known about it when I heard Mussolini declare war to America... I was in Piazza Venezia, shocked by the announcement. America entering the War! ...That was the beginning of a real war for us in Rome. We heard later of Pearl Harbor, the Japanese version of it...."

Pressed by his questions, I told him of the War in Rome, of Kesselring's reign of terror, of our men hidden in the hospitals and the catacombs, of the German soldiers I helped desert and of how the Gestapo arrested Bona and me and how the deserters, once found, were abandoned to themselves by the Italian Resistance, something I discovered after I was arrested by the Germans. It didn't seem strange to speak to a man I hardly knew and who had no experience of war in his own land of those far away events which were buried for me by now beyond a wide fearsome Ocean and four years of American war for survival. Indeed, I told him things I had never told anybody before, of the death of my father when I was five and of life with my mother and three small siblings in the German-speaking beautiful Merano during twenty years of Fascism, of our flight to Rome at the onset of the War, of my Greek boyfriend and of the ultimate humiliation I had suffered from the *Hauptsturmführer* who had arrested me. I told him of my life with Claude in Italy and in America and of Bona's and Eddie's arrival, of the College of St. Elizabeth in New Jersey and of my interview at Barnard....

Ray seemed to be thirsty for everything that concerned my life as if he had wanted to have lived it himself, and I felt completely at home revealing to him my most intimate feelings.

He listened with an intensity that surprised me, his arm around my shoulders covered by his jacket. It was dark and peaceful around us when he began to talk about himself in a natural way as if what had happened to him on this side of the Ocean had something to do with what had happened to me on the other side. As if we had indeed lived our lives side by side.

"My own war," he laughed, "was fought in the Pentagon. Yes, I helped our Army fight against you, but as you said, it was all for the best."

And he told me of the type of research he carried out as a mathematician, how far away he felt, while he was working, from the real war I had experienced. I could feel while he talked that at certain moments, he was anxious.

By now, there was complete silence around us, cut at moments by the boats on the Hudson. The traffic on the Drive had almost stopped. We were alone.

"I had my own war to fight," he laughed suddenly, "annoying, tedious, personal. My war was at home...." He spoke in a low voice, almost to himself, of long years before and after the birth of his children, interminable years in which his wife had been very closely involved with a colleague, a very well-known colleague whom he grew to despise. The two families had lived through the years almost as one, the two wives' intimate friends. At certain moments, if I understood well, the two lovers acted as they did with his consent. At others, there were requests and pledges to stop that went unfulfilled. During one of his wife's trips to Norway, he had himself grown close to the divorced wife of a colleague who took care of his twins, but he refused to divorce and to marry her after his wife's return.

At this very moment, he concluded with an air of resignation, there was truce and forgiveness. Both he and his wife had suffered enough. They longed for peace. For this reason, he was so grateful for my generous attitude towards Else, for receiving her as a student and for being her friend. She was well aware of how he felt towards me, but she really liked me.

As we got up from the bench to go home, each in a different direction, I felt as close to Ray as a human being can be close to another. I did not ask myself any question. As I was about to get into my car parked in front of Milbank Hall, Ray put his arm around me again and held me tight, close to him. He had tears in his eyes.

During the Spring of 1952, Ray and I entered our private earthly Paradise within a Columbia I was learning fast to redimension. Like two atoms once separated that collided by chance into one another again, we rejoiced at first without any thought of boundaries or feeling of guilt. There was no room for thought. Once we had read together the first awesome line of the magic book, there was no alternative for us but to continue reading it together. The feeling of ineluctability was shared by both. It didn't bother me. What bothered me was the censure of society around us that targeted each of us for a different reason.

It was Ray himself who made me aware of one aspect of our situation that had escaped me: society surrounding us, had they discovered our relationship, would have harshly disapproved of it and would have tried to punish us for it. I was, he noted, far more vulnerable to society's disapproval and punishment than he was. I should never forget that I was an Assistant Professor without tenure. Tenderly but implacably, like a doctor with his patient, Ray made me think of my official position at Barnard in all of its moral weakness, until I felt it like a stigma. The thought, when it fell upon me, frightened and angered me. Most of the time, however, for some reason that I cannot explain, I lived without fears in my dangerous nirvana. I loved my job. Why should I be judged on any other basis but on my own performance at work?

Else came often to my office. Ray had appraised her of the development of our relationship. Her admiration and affection for me were in no way diminished by her knowledge of the facts. At times, to my surprise, she seemed almost grateful for my presence near her husband.

"I have hurt him badly through the years," she would confess, sitting in the old armchair in front of my desk, "but it was beyond my power to control. He is a wonderfully generous man whom I deeply admire and love, but...."

Without my prompting her, Else gave me her own very detailed version of how, shortly following her arrival in America as a young woman from Norway, she had met the eminent Professor, Ray's colleague, who soon became her lover, while Ray, in spite of his wonderful intentions, had neglected her, lost as he was in his own research.... She told me how she and her lover over the years had been overwhelmed by a most passionate and anguishing relationship, while his wife was kept unaware of it. Ray, she admitted, had generally been aware of it and when at one point had "re-discovered" it, had been generous enough to forgive.... A thick packet of correspondence in French that witnessed the long anguishing romance had unfortunately fallen one day by chance into Ray's hands, when Ray was teaching summer school in a scorching New York City and Else and the children were vacationing with her lover's family. Ray had once again forgiven. On the other hand, he had had his own love affair while she was in Norway one summer with her most intimate girlfriend who, upon Else's return, had followed Ray to the Pentagon in Washington, begging him to marry her. Ray had refused not only for the sake of the children but out of sensitivity towards Else. There was nothing Ray could do under the circumstances which she wouldn't forgive. She wished him happiness, the happiness he had not found in the family.

I grew so interested in Else's story, mostly because of its complexity, that I wished I could have followed it more objectively. But, alas, I couldn't, because, as winter gave way to spring and spring to summer, I found myself caught in a web of my own, which was partially her own web, a web which was such an absolute novelty in my own life that at times I wished I could fly back from the Columbia campus to the blessed garden of the Nuns of Charity in New Jersey. But I couldn't. I was by now chained to Columbia by a double chain....

The days were getting longer. With the mild breezes of an early spring the contorted branches of the giant trees along the Hudson melted into a new form of life. Winter's stark, velvet orange sunsets gave way to the tender azure skies of April with white clouds sailing lazily over the river. Then the cherry trees in the park blossomed and the linden trees along College Walk began to release their acute fragrance. Students and faculty strolled from the Drive into the Park. Couples, young and not so young, held hands and expressed in public that amount of affection that society at that time allowed them.

Ray insisted, quite rightly so, that we obey all rules of public decorum. Thus, I discovered to my dismay that no sooner had we entered our private paradise that I was asked to behave like an Eve who had committed a mortal sin for which humanity, women in particular, had to suffer *in aeternum* or at least up to the end of history.

My position, Ray explained to me, was most delicate. We worked in a women's College whose Dean—at that time Barnard did not have as yet a President—was a Quaker. She had just replaced a great spinster by the name of Virginia who spelled 'virginity' for the women who worked in her enclave. I had already brought too much attention on myself by engaging as actors the cream of the faculty in the performance of Eduardo de Filippo's play, *Napoli Milionaria*, the play I had originally planned to launch, with my husband Claude, on Broadway after I landed on American soil.

The performance had been an immense success, I answered his objections. It had brought to Columbia a bit of Europe in the original. The Barnard administration had been pleasantly taken by the daring enterprise. Everybody had been duly shaken at the end of the play by the howling of the firemen's sirens that mimicked the sirens that shook Naples under bombs. They seemed to tear the building apart. "*C'est la guerre à Barnard!*" ("It is war at Barnard!") commented the then chairman of the French department, a stately gentleman who resembled De Gaulle. He had been the Chairman of the Search Committee responsible for my presence on campus. But Ray was inexorable. Didn't I remember that it was he, Ray, who brought the sirens on campus? He saw some kind of symbolism in that act which escaped me. My colleagues, men as well as women, loved me, I said. He frowned. Yes, but precisely because they loved me, I should beware.

During the spring of 1952, Ray wanted to make sure that the two of us behaved in such a way as not to allow the homely Barnard society a chance to envisage possible connections between his role in *Napoli Milionaria* and his real life. I therefore agreed with him to some strict rules and regulations that he invented for us, like holding hands being forbidden between 110th and 125th Street. Nobody should be allowed to suspect that the blond mathematician had any non-respectable relationship with the Italian Assistant Professor who was by now everybody's friend on campus. As I think about it now at the distance of so many years, I conclude he was right.

Ray should not have worried. Nobody divined anything improper going on between us. Only two people were informed of everything: my sister Bona and of course Ray's wife Else. Neither of the two disapproved.

In our after-dinner conversations, Bona was always delighted to hear more about the blond mathematician. It was, I guess, for her like following a soap opera, an escape into the blue from her otherwise dreary life.

Else kept on attending my classes. Her Italian soon became so good I could have transferred her to "Intermediate Italian." I did not do so for obvious reasons. Yet she spoke and wrote almost as well as her husband. There was in fact a kind of contest going on between the two, a contest in 'language' and in getting the most of my "friendship." While Ray had stopped writing to me altogether, Else took to writing long and charming compositions which were for me a joy to read.

March gave way to April. The trees in the Barnard "Jungle" were all in bloom. The magnolia displayed then as it does today its fleshy pink and purple petals, more a fruit than a flower. After class Else at times would sit in my office and spontaneously answer questions I had never asked. She would sit in the old armchair, which I had by now cleared from the overflow of books and memorabilia of the deceased spinster and would open her heart to me with a touching sincerity. Out of my office windows trucks made their way as they do today with a roaring rumble up Broadway, while Else unraveled, without any restraint or effort, her anguishing story of love and pain, almost of love and death, which had taken place in the past years.

What endeared Else to me was that I was not shocked by her story. I was overwhelmed and she instinctively felt it. There is a special channel of communication between two women who find themselves under extraordinary circumstances. The unsaid breathes into what is said, it makes it rise and ferment through mysterious channels. Soon a powerful picture of human passion and deep suffering stood in front of my eyes. More than a picture it was a drama. Around the two central characters who held the stage constantly, other two minor characters suffered perhaps just as much, with the disadvantage that they didn't love, therefore, they did not take initiative in acting. Part of their suffering was due indeed to their being confined permanently to the role of minor characters. Thus, they could speak only when the protagonists allowed them to do so. They were in sum confined to reactions.

Ray, in this story, was confined most of the time, although not always, to reactions. This pained me. It pained Else too. In fact, it was pain that induced Else to welcome my entering on stage almost as part of her own drama. What remained to be seen but was never mentioned was the role I was destined to take: action or reaction? While Else sat in the old armchair in a light summer dress that revealed her beautiful muscular body under the thin cotton cloth, I was not aware of what my own role would be in the passionate inter-relation of four human beings, three of them members of the faculty of Barnard and Columbia. I was overwhelmed by her drama and she, reacting to my heartfelt sympathy, found a shelter within my sympathy like a tired animal who has run aimlessly for too long.

When, in the evening, I reported Else's and her lover's drama to Bona, I projected it without wanting to into the medieval frame of Abélard and Eloïse, filtered through nineteenth century French novels, since the two protagonists spoke and wrote to each other only in French. Upper Broadway at Morningside Heights acquired then the colors of Paris' Old Latin Quarter. Perhaps it was Bona's passionate reaction that made me dramatize the story: a web of illicit loves within the *licitum*!

April gave way to May. With their inebriating fragrance, the flowers of the linden trees on College Walk evoked the alleys of my little Alpine hometown, Merano, through which, as an adolescent, I used to walk happily on my way to school with my siblings and friends. At times, my sisters and I would dive with our hands into the thick foliage of those linden trees to search for June bugs (*Maykäfer* or *maggiolini*), which we would later free during a boring class of Latin grammar in the eighteenth-century convent which, in 1918, had become an Italian *Liceo*. However, if by any chance, as we were walking under the linden trees, the silhouette of my favorite professor on whom I had a secret crush would glide by in the distance, I was caught by an uneasy feeling. In order to avoid him seeing me blush from head to toe, I would suddenly turn away. So now, on College walk, like a bird caught in a web, if I saw Ray in the distance I would turn around as fast as I could in order not to show my embarrassment.

As May triumphed on College Walk and classes were about to end, I felt at times painfully caught in the spider web of those illicit academic loves whose stories might have filled my office and slowly invaded my classroom. Instinctively, I rebelled against the feeling. While my wings were being slowly and imperceptibly caught within thin, impalpable threads, I nostalgically recalled at times the pure, child-like joy of that golden Fall when, having entered my Earthly Paradise as a free Eve, I had never envisaged a disturbance would cloud the Olympus I was allowed to share with the gods. Was my freedom gone forever? There was a tragic aspect to Else's drama. The moment I began living within it, it lost the golden tinsel of literature. It became real life and it hurt. Was I to be caught into a web very much like the one she was in, and one that would also hurt?

Disintegration of Dreams

In June 1952, Else left with the children to spend the summer in Norway. During the spring I had often visited with the family. I loved the three children and the children loved me. My four-year old Claudia played happily with Ray's seven-year old twins. Before leaving, Else spoke to me quietly. She was happy to leave, she said, a bit worried perhaps. Yet she blindly trusted Ray in my hands. Did she think that I could be trusted? She knew I had sympathized with her own personal tragedy. Did she really trust Ray? I don't know. Perhaps what she trusted was the pain that awaited us all....

The year 1952 was my fourth summer in America. It was a very hot one. The pavement on Broadway gave way under one's feet. College Walk was almost empty. During the summer in 1950, that is before I entered Barnard, I had managed to take Claude and Claudia to Italy with my own money. What a cozy feeling it had been to live cramped in a small villa in Anzio, surrounded by my old family, listening to the sea while Claudia and my sister Francesca's children built castles in the sand. How sweet to evoke at night the years of the war with Francesca. We lived then in the shade of the Roman pines and of the oleanders' bitter-smelling flowers. Anzio and Rome were so different from the year of the Allied Landing. At times I thought it wasn't me who had lived there during the War. Summer had been bitter-sweet on the Mediterranean shores.

Until 1952 I had thought that summer in New York was hardly bearable. Summer 1952 changed my perspective on the world beyond Gibraltar and the one in which I lived. New York in the summer of 1952 was a simmering, pitiless cauldron of boiling lava. It was hot inside the buildings. New York buildings, I rapidly discovered, were poorly built, impenetrable to the sea breeze. With the shades down to keep the sun out, a fan could raise a faint, very faint breeze in the hot room: a sweet noise like the buzzing of a bee.

I listened to the thumping of Ray's heart. There was a crack in the ceiling above us, a picture on the wall of Ray when he was five years old in Frankfurt.

"Are you sleeping, Ray?" I asked. With his right arm he drew me close to him and kissed me. He pushed me slightly aside to look at me, blue eyes twinkling with gentle irony: "You are beautiful. More beautiful than ever and I love you." Then he got up and moved to the piano. Chopin filled my world.

On August 15, after summer school ended, Ray led Claude, Claudia, Bona, Eddie and myself for a week-long vacation on Crystal Lake in New Hampshire.

"*Ecco il nostro New Hampshire*" ("Here is our New Hampshire"), Ray wrote on a picture of a young Ray at the prow of a boat, a camera hanging from a leather strap across his shoulders, the shadow of a smile, hair blown by the wind. There is a cryptic message in the back of the photo: "*Ecco il nostro Crystal Lake. T.V.M.B.*" ("Here is our Crystal Lake"). Under T.V.M.B ("*ti voglio molto bene*"—'I love you very much') a brief note says: "*La fontana da sempre la sua acqua anche quando tu non puoi bere*" ("The fountain always gives water even when you cannot drink").

There are a few other traces of our lives from the spring and summer of 1952 besides this picture and this note. In another envelope there are three pictures—one of myself, slim and tanned, in a black bathing suit on the dock of a lake; one of the two of us sitting together reading a letter from Else in Norway. The third picture is of myself near a lake with a cute four-year old on my shoulders.

Our New Hampshire. Ray had carved out the two of us from the surrounding world. The cryptogram *"Ti voglio molto bene"* was as much as he would put in writing. *"La prudenza non è mai troppa"* ("You can never be too prudent") as the old proverb states. Ray sent me the pictures in September after Else's return. I guess he didn't dare to keep them at home.

***

Crystal Lake was the place where Ray had vacationed with his family for two years. Before then he would vacation in picturesque Hudson Valley farms with another family which had been very close to his wife since he had brought her to America from Oslo in 1938. I guess that bringing me and my family to Crystal Lake signaled for him the beginning of a new life. Consciously or unconsciously, he had led me to a place that was particularly meaningful to him.

Perhaps he thought of my family as his own. It was a fact that he was never jealous of Claude while I was jealous of Else. And why did my own family accept my proposal to spend one week with Ray at Crystal Lake? Only Bona was aware of my relation to Ray and did not disapprove of it. Everything "American" puzzled her.

If I were a historian, I would search for some rational reasons for what happened. But I am not a historian. All I can point to in the mist of the past is the fact that Claude and I had both been in the process of fighting to become a "family on American soil," each of us fresh from the experience of the War, when my own personal life suddenly changed. All movement towards unity stopped at that moment, for no particular apparent reason, except perhaps because at the center of the process I felt that it was I alone who had tried to create, on this side of the Atlantic, something analogous to the family fortress my mother had built upon the ashes of the first World War, brick upon brick, all on her own, with her four children. Now place, time, and circumstances did not seem to be in our favor. When I gave up trying to keep our entire family together, everyone in my family stopped gravitating towards unity. A process of disintegration was set off that only I could have stopped. I did not.

Why I did not stop it I can only guess. The feeling of emptiness I had felt for years in America had given way to an overwhelming and irreplaceable feeling of life fed by a relationship with a passionate, intelligent, and handsome man. After forty years of life with Ray and years after his physical disappearance from this earth, I still feel, at times, Ray's presence near me as I felt it during those interminable pale blue sunsets on Crystal Lake or during the moonless nights when our elegant rustic pine cabin swallowed by a thick forest echoed the music of Rachmaninoff and Tchaikovsky, the music Ray had brought with him to Crystal Lake. At night, when we swam in those crystal waters, that music had followed us, a faint breeze in the air.

At Crystal Lake I sensed without admitting it to myself that it was with Ray I had to build my family, no matter how painful and difficult the process. I see it better now, as the distance of over forty years from the event lends me the proper perspective.

At Crystal Lake a metamorphosis began taking place within me over which I had no control and of which I was most of the time unaware. Consequently, not only did I not attempt in any way to stop the process of family disintegration which had begun long before Crystal Lake, but with time I provoked it. This happened through two years of painful crisis in which I often felt overwhelmed, prey to events, incapable of gaining any form of control over my own life, of steering my boat in any direction.

Mid-September 1952. As soon as the ship brought Else and the children back from Norway, I thought that "the Spring had stopped running." Hence Ray's words accompanying the pictures of Crystal Lake assumed for me an extraordinary meaning.

In reality, after Else's return from Norway, I could not believe my eyes. Ray's main reference point became his household. He took up the role of husband and father in such a gentle, firm and convincing way that it took all my passionate belief in him not to give in to utter despair, although I knew I could only expect despair.

At first, I tried to accommodate. After all, Else had been my friend all throughout the spring. I loved Ray's children. The relationship between Ray and Else had not changed. It was now what it had always been and what it was when we first met. It had allowed Ray to "make room for me" within the space that his marriage consented. His marriage consented to a great deal. Yet it was a *marriage* with everything that that simple fact implied.

Then I rebelled. After the intimacy of that marvelous summer I could not and would not accept the *space* consented to me by his marriage. I wanted him within another space. What kind of space I didn't know. But at this point it didn't matter.

I also became aware that Ray, my beloved Ray, did not in fact have "an iron constitution" but rather "a constitution made of reeds and bamboo sticks that consented only to a moderate amount of pressure," as he wrote to John von Neumann who had asked him to be his assistant, a prestigious position which he declined because of its extraordinary professional pressures. When this new realization came into the picture, I suddenly became sadly conscious that by putting "pressure" on him, with my rashness or despair, I would run the risk of losing him forever.

This was at the time the greatest risk I could run because our love had rapidly become an essential element of my own equilibrium. By losing him I would lose a part of myself, the best part—my joy of living. I became aware that life is nothing if not joy of living, desire to live.

To make things worse, trapped within an intricate net of conflicting emotions, I was confined by the environment in which I lived to a constant and thorough use of *prudentia*, of the use of wisdom not to live a better life but only to survive within the narrow space allowed me by conventions. Trapped by my emotions, I was forced by circumstances to continue my friendly relationship with Ray's family, more than ever before desirous of Ray's personal attention. I gradually learned to hate my Earthly Paradise. At times I cursed it as if it had bitterly deceived me. I would have indeed rejected it as real Hell, had it not been for my students and colleagues. Through my suffering I slowly learned to redimension the Columbia campus, to lower it from the heavenly heights in which my imagination had lifted it and bring it to a human level, a space in which human beings lived exercising the same profession as I did. We were teaching together, administering together the institution so that it may work as we wanted it. I fully enjoyed it because it went much beyond the books I had read during the German occupation, when I felt it was up to me to choose whether to turn East or West. It was real life democracy.

By this time, Ray was no longer attending my course, nor was Else. My classrooms became my own kingdom, a refuge at times from my miseries, more often the place where I could be myself as I had never been at Barnard. Free skies with no ecstasies but at least with a feeling of satisfaction for what I was able to achieve on my own in a little corner of the campus.

My repressed desire also found another outlet: the written word. An outpouring of letters and poems, some short and amusing, some of them answered by Ray with brief and witty notes began in September 1952 and continued. The most telling compositions deal with his philosophy of *prudentia*. Ray had warned in the past about the virtue of *prudentia* in the most clear terms: and I finally felt upset by his argument.

"Sweet Maristella—I write to you in Italian in order to tell you that you are my sweet woman and I love you very, very much. Naturally in the company of others, I cannot show my love for you. We must not show that I leave with you, for instance, or come into a room with you. People would guess we were together. They could guess the time we spent together. As I have explained to you many times, I cannot and do not want to proceed that way. Then everything that goes on between you and me could be seen as through a telescope. But when we are alone you will see what I think of you. Don't you understand? So I write to you in Italian and in secret this short note without anybody knowing it. It is sweet to write in secret—like for a child to eat his candy in secret. If I am indeed the thread that leads you into the world, please trust the thread and be a little less unhappy and do not worry about my family. Because I love you deeply. You are my little woman. I caress you. Your R."

The letter made me furious.

Lavinium Lavinio Lavinia

The very personal memories of Crystal Lake were slowly becoming a dream after a ship from Norway in September brought Else back to the campus, when all of a sudden another escape from reality rose on my horizon. I helped the Lorches to find a house at a beach near Rome for the summer preceding the opening of the University of Rome at which Ray had been invited to spend a year teaching while on sabbatical. It was a little house near my family's home in Lavinio. Lavinio was a newly built, popular hamlet on the shores of the Tyrrhenian Sea near Rome. My sister Francesca had been one of the first to build a house in Lavinio, and the whole family enjoyed it.

Lavinio had first come to my attention before the landing of Allied troops in 1944. It had existed for me since shortly before the liberation of Rome because of my professional connections with Virgil's *Aeneid* which I had taught, year in year out during the War, at the *Liceo Virgilio*. My colleague at the *Virgilio*, Vinci Verginelli, who taught with me the parallel section on Virgil, had explored along with me the areas surrounding Rome that were mentioned in the poem.

I treasure pictures of students surrounding me on the Colli Albani where Cicero, whose letters we also read in class, had built more than one villa. Reading Virgil we were attracted by a beach called *Lavinio*, immortalized by Virgil from Book VI to Book XII of the *Aeneid* in honor of the Emperor Augustus. To be sure, there were no ruins in Lavinio to remind us of Virgilian stories. Lavinio was then, as it is today, a perfect arch of sandy beach sweetly descending from a *pineta* of Roman pines to a blue sea. The students loved our escapades to the beach and so did we, their teachers. They had learned by heart passages from the *Aeneid,* where Virgil described the legendary past of Lavinium, and how King Latinus had graciously received the shipwrecked Aeneas, survivor of a burning Troy, who had finally reached the shores of Italy after months of sailing the Mediterranean. Through the last six books of the *Aeneid* Virgil sings of how King Latinus after a harsh war with his neighbors gave his first daughter Lavinia in marriage to Aeneas, much to the dismay of his wife Amata who had planned to see Lavinia marrying the greatest local warrior, Turnus. In the Virgilian legend Romulus, founder of Rome, boasts of Princess Lavinia as his first and most important ancestor. It was the legend relived in Virgil's words in a Roman classroom (at times under Allied bombardments) that had attracted all of us to the deserted beach not far from Rome that was called *Lavinio.*

I remember a great silence around us, as we sat together, students and teachers alike, under the bluest skies, on the beach of a *Lavinium* created by the poet, enjoying a day of freedom from a Rome crushed by hunger and fear of death. Bread, salami, and wine were provided by the students' families that lived on the nearby farms. Yet what mattered for us at the time was Virgil's marvelous story which we read aloud in Latin.

While the Lorches spent the summer at a rented house in Lavinio, I stayed with my sister Francesca, visiting with Ray and Else frequently. Rome being nearby, I took one or both of them to the city on a regular basis. One day, while Ray and I were in Rome and Else, bored to death, was sunning herself alongside my sister Francesca on the silky sand of Lavinio, she suddenly burst out into an open accusation of my "stealing her husband from her." She told Francesca from beginning to end the whole story of her life in New York, in the environment of Barnard-Columbia and, within the story, she revealed the dangerous role I had played so far and would probably continue to play near her husband. It was in my best interest and that of my career, she added, that I should, in her view, give up my affair with her husband and trust myself and my own potential in the new environment by myself.

Else's revelation did not produce in Francesca the reaction she expected. Francesca listened, she told me later, adding that she trusted me completely. After Else's revelation, my family and I reduced to the minimum our visits to the Lorches. The tension between me and the Lorches in Lavinio increased without my noticing during the month of August and September as I turned to my past life in Rome as if I had never left it. Lavinio in this sense performed a real miracle for me as I spent the whole month of September in Rome connecting with scholars and institutions that I felt were potentially open to exchanges with us overseas. At the end of September my voyage alone with Claudia by train from Rome to Rotterdam was an unexpected discovery of a "Europe" I had forgotten, overwhelmed as I was by my passion for Ray. I fully enjoyed Europe from the train and Claudia did as well. She was particularly taken by the Rhine when I told her the story of Lorelei and, having a facility for languages, she learned the poem by heart in German. As for my Ocean crossing, my voyage on the *Sibajak* with Dutch emigrants forced to emigrate to Canada because of the flooding of their land led me back to a better understanding of how to take advantage of the new world where I lived. I became aware of my intense desire to help Western Europe in the best possible way.

Arriving at Barnard without Ray, who now was teaching in Italy for the year, did not produce the effects I feared. Lavinio had indeed accomplished a change in me which I did not expect. Happy to write to Ray almost daily the results of the work I engaged in, I was indeed delighted with the unexpected freedom I enjoyed without Ray's presence.

Back in New York, in my daily letters to Ray I communicated with pride my rapid diving into the life of Barnard and Columbia. I began by connecting my own little department of Italian with the rest of the University and by opening doors and windows to inter-departmental cooperation. I accepted the invitation of Professor Barry Ulanov, the most popular teacher of the Barnard English department, to teach with him an interdepartmental course which covered mainly French and Russian literature with some clear ties to Italian and English literature of the nineteenth century. By common agreement we named the course "Romantic Agony."

As for my own little department at Barnard, inspired by Eliot's "Four Quartets" with which I fell in love as soon as they were published, I focused my teaching on Dante, a kind of Dante in English *à la Eliot*. With the years, that particular interdisciplinary course was to become *Dante's World* team-taught by three professors alongside myself from the fields of history, art history, and theology. As such it evolved as the foundation for a "Medieval and Renaissance Program" supported a few years later by an NEH grant to Barnard. The medieval historian Susan Wemple was my first partner in the course and in the creation of the Program. *Dante's World* remained a most popular course given in English until my retirement in 1990, at which time the Dean of Barnard abolished it.

In November 1953, Dean Peardon called my attention to a very special case which focused on Professor Enrico De Negri, a famous philosopher and Dante Scholar who had been chosen by a Columbia Committee to replace the retiring Italian Department Chairman, the well-known Dantist Dino Bigongiari. Enrico De Negri had called upon himself the enmity of Professors Riccio and Marraro, the two Italian Americans who dominated the department at Columbia College and General Studies, but he enjoyed the support of the English department at Columbia. The "fight for De Negri" ended quietly with an invitation by Professor Ferruolo for him to join the Berkeley department of Italian, the most renowned at the time in North America. Riccio then turned to me suddenly with an interesting offer which surprised me: Would I take over his graduate course in Italian which appeared in the catalogue under his name? He must have felt uncomfortable in it. I accepted the offer without discussion and enjoyed teaching the course, while

Professor Marraro at General Studies employed Olga Ragusa, who had recently obtained a brilliant Ph.D. in Italian Modern and Contemporary Literature. Ragusa and I joined hands with reciprocal satisfaction.

Fortune Pope, Chairman of the Italian-American committee for the Casa Italiana's financing, then bluntly asked me to take over the direction of the theater of the Casa Italiana. The Casa Italiana was the Columbia building founded in the early 1920's and funded by three wealthy Italian Americans desirous that Italy not be the only European country which did not have a "house" on campus. I, of course, accepted with pleasure. I do not remember precisely when and how Marta Abba, Pirandello's favorite actress, his mistress and literary executor, turned to me with the request to take the leading role in the playwright's *La vita che ti diedi* *("*The Life I gave you*")*. The play's success encouraged Professor Anne Paolucci, a star in English literature and founder of the Pirandello Society, to ask me to direct the Pirandello Society which focuses on the research and presentation of plays by Pirandello in the United States.

Ray was of course delighted by my letters in which love suddenly took an ancillary role to other interests of mine. His own letters were equally filled with details of his intense activities not limited to Italy but expanded through the half of Europe called Western Europe after the treaty of Yalta in 1944 had divided Europe in two. As I detailed my "achievements" in my daily letters, I did not forget to point out that under Professor Paul Oskar Kristeller's direction I pursued without interruption the critical edition of Valla's work *On Pleasure* for whose publication I had signed a contract in Milan in 1947. Else had typed for me the three hundred folios of a manuscript of the Vatican Library that I had copied during the War.

The Blessings born of Courage

In view of what happened in my life on campus after my return from Rome in September of 1953, the episode of "Lavinio" signaled a radical evolution in my relationship with Ray. I moved from depending on the precariousness of an illicit, destructive love to embracing a new independence.

In May 1954, while still in New York, before returning to Europe once again, I stopped writing to Ray. My last letter was #157. His last was #57. Perhaps the imbalance had finally dawned on me. During the year Ray spent in Italy with his family I must have become increasingly aware of the price I was paying to pursue my love dream at the moment: my own peace of mind. I had left Europe in order to live. Living meant building. Yet now what I learned was the impossibility of our building together. Lavinio signaled the direction our relationship would have to take in the future: if there was to be any continuation of our relationship, we would have to unite to build together a family in the literal and in the metaphorical sense.

As the summer of 1954 approached, the anguishing experience of Lavinio haunted me as did the many months that I spent on the American side of the Atlantic, working assiduously at maintaining a connection across an ocean, a connection that seemed to dissolve as quickly as I forged it. I had originally agreed with Ray to see him again briefly during the summer of 1954 while I would be teaching in Florence. But in May I stopped writing. Perhaps I was afraid of pursuing what I felt existed only in my mind: a deeper, more committed relationship than we actually had at the time. I stopped writing almost without noticing it. May, a crazy May in New York, was followed for me by a delightful week with the "family" (Claudia, Claude, Bona, and Eddie) in a lonely cabin in Northern Maine, absorbing every drop of the environment's savage beauty. From there I wrote to Ray only once, making him read, between the lines, that I was setting myself free. Then, in Quebec with Claudia and Claude I boarded a Panamanian ship loaded with students. After sailing through the Saint Lawrence estuary, we crossed the Ocean. To pay for our trip I worked all day organizing life on board. Never did a crossing seem shorter and happier.

In Paris, then in Bern, finally in Florence, where my job as a mentor hired by Barnard took me, I found many anguished messages from Ray at the American Express Office: he wanted me to keep my promise and to see him in Europe. The roles had now been reversed. He was the one longing for the meeting. Within me there was a silence that I did not question.

In July, I was teaching Barnard students in the heart of the old city of Florence, in Via Ghibellina, off Piazza Santa Croce, in the palace that had been the birthplace of Amerigo Vespucci. Of the three Barnard students all but one had succumbed to a brief but fatal contact with charming Florentine males, mainly on motorcycles. While my students literally disappeared, my personal pride remained intact, as I held court reading Dante and illustrating contemporary Euro-American relations to a young European elite that had arrived from Oxford along with one young American, Mona Tobin, my major in Italian.

As Fulbright lecturer in Europe in 1953, Ray had been independently building his own Euro-American partnership on the solid foundation of his mathematical research, more precisely on Banach Spaces. In July 1954, he was pursuing a mathematical vacation with his family, in a villa in Beaulieu on the Côte d'Azure, close to a "Bourbakiste" French collaborator.

Reacting to Ray's insistent appeals, I called him up one night from Paris at the number of a hotel in Beaulieu that he had given me. I was relieved by the feeling of freedom I experienced while waiting for the *garçon* to call him from his villa: I did not try to imagine the environment in which he lived nor what the call might bring about in our lives. In calling him, I was simply answering an instinct I did not question.

That night over the phone it was agreed that we would meet in Genova, half way between Florence and Beaulieu. The conversation focused on practical details: the date and the place.

Key decisions are taken under extraordinary conditions. Genova became the setting for a vision which was an act of folly in the positive and creative sense of the word. An act of creative folly celebrates a special wisdom within which peace co-exists with conflict. Our Genova experience of 1954 made us aware that an individual takes perhaps one and only one decision in his or her life. All life depends on it.

On the old desk in New York, freed of all papers, there are many smiling faces looking at me from the infinite dimensions of old pictures. In one of them, taken on New Year's Eve 1989, Ray is surrounded by our three girls and myself. Within three months, he would complete his destiny on earth. Within the other frames on Ray's old desk, there is a picture of myself that every visitor mistakes for Lavinia. Framed in worn-out, brown leather, adorned with intricate squares of turquoise, I stand *mezzo busto, di profilo*, slightly smiling. My hair is thick, brown, and wavy. I wear a black linen blouse that leaves my shoulders half bare, silver earrings and a silver and coral necklace, Ray's most recent gifts. I hold a red rose to my lips and look off into the distance. The picture is so faded that only the black has maintained its natural color. It looks like a Renaissance painting in need of restoration. A woman with a wide striped skirt in the background tells me that Ray took the picture in the marketplace in Genova in 1954. Having lived so long with the occupants on Ray's old desk, this picture has by now become part of the desk itself. It grows old with it and with me.

On my marquetry desk there is one picture, framed in old silver and velvet, resting among many other family pictures: Ray and I stand close to each other with me leaning against an overturned boat. Behind us is the perfect curve of a port where many boats lull in the summer heat. This picture is also quite faded: small and thin, I am wearing a long skirt and a pink blouse, my hair gathered in a kerchief. I hardly reach up to Ray's shoulders. He stands, his right arm around me, a bit bent, his thumb on his belt, tall, blond, handsome, hair blown by the wind. We both look off into the distance with a faint smile. This picture, known to the family as "the Portofino picture," is a universally recognized witness to the fact that when Ray and I met we were a handsome couple. It is also proof that something happened in Portofino and, of course, in Genova. What is the untold story behind the faint smiles of those faded pictures?

On a very hot day in August 1954, I departed from Florence at noon. I had informed my students at Via Ghibellina that I would be absent for a few days. No one knew where I was going. They must have thought I was going to Rome to see my family. At the Stazione Centrale in Florence I bought a round trip ticket to Genova. The long ride on a slow train allowed me to enjoy the passing view of villages perched like castles atop olive-dotted hills and long, cypress-lined alleys. The train moved on through Tuscany and eastern Liguria skirting the high mountains that had not as yet, in 1954, been pierced by tunnels. At the bottom of every bay lay a quaint little village. At one point, after many hot hours spent mostly at the open window trying to protect my eyes from specks of flying coal from the smokestack of the locomotive, a wide, sweeping view of a city appeared in the distance. The white buildings looked like a sheet spread on a rock. As we approached, the city's blue port came into view, with its big boats loading and unloading passengers and merchandise.

The train stopped at the Stazione Principe. I stepped off, carrying my small bag, and looked around. I did not know what to expect. I felt more hollow inside than anxious. The station was almost empty. It was very hot. From the far end of the platform I recognized Ray moving towards me. I noticed a bouquet of red carnations in his hands. "I have been standing here for hours," he said, "enough for these flowers to wilt. Two trains came in from Florence. I was about to give up hope."

The flowers were indeed drooping. He told me he loved railway stations. As he led me out of the station, he pointed to the architectural harmony of the hall. Hand in hand, we moved into the Piazza, closed in by the buildings, almost empty and silent. A heavy heat hung over it. The wide hall of the old Majestic Colombo Hotel, facing the station, welcomed us with the elegance of an old Mediterranean first-class lodging: huge marble columns, marble floors, palms, and a soft light filtering in through the windows. It was silent and sleepy. I handed over my American passport at the reception desk. The clerk assigned me to a room on the top floor. Ray's room was on the floor below mine. My room was small with a small white bed in a corner, a table and an armchair.

We opened the shutters in my *mansarde* and we both trembled with delight. Our hotel hung perpendicularly over the port. Its heavy fragrance of fish and salt wafted into the room. Large and small boats rested immobile on the water that mirrored a light blue sky. The city entered the room softly through the open window with a whiff of heavy, bluish air. The city belonged to us and we belonged to it. We embraced.

After the sun set over the port of Genova, the Piazza della Stazione and the dark alleys of the old port became a beehive within which only an inexperienced observer could say that the bees flitted about aimlessly. The port throbbed with a life that obeyed its own rules. We were immediately swallowed by it.

Hand in hand, we walked through the narrow alleys of the port and absorbed their smell. Tired of walking, we sat in a corner of a tavern and enjoyed all kinds of fish and vegetables, bread and wine. We spoke of theorems. Pencil in hand, Ray demonstrated the Pythagorean theorem to me while near us a fisherman looked on bemused. "*Matematica,*" he commented, "*la mia passione*" ("Mathematics, my passion"). "*Anche la mia*" ("Mine too"), Ray added with a smile. We agreed that mathematics was music and poetry. Harmony, said Ray. When we walked out, we took the paper napkin with us.

We wandered about the port. People talked to us as if we were part of their lives, and indeed we were. We sat atop a pile of rope cables between the riggings of the boats, a slice of pale moon smiling down on us. The silent night ended in harmony with dawn. The sun rose over the boats, a clear bluish pink. As the day moved on, it became unbearably hot. The afternoon was heavy with the silence of muffled voices and laughter, filtering through the heavy sheet of haze that enveloped the port and the city. When the sun set, the voices became louder, a concert of voices, hands interweaving, women with wide skirts rustling, men hustling after them. A pale moon hung over the port of

Genova for the two nights we were there, until the sun overshadowed it.

The day before we left Genova, we took a local *trenino* ("little train") to Santa Margherita Ligure. From there we went by carriage to Portofino. Santa Margherita was a sleepy, middle-class resort town, white villas buried under purple avalanches of bougainvillea, alleys of palm trees, hotels fit for a Visconti film.

I don't remember whether the idea of the carriage was Ray's, mine, or both of ours. The horses trotted slowly along the sea, on a road without cars, high above the rocks. Stretches of blue water popped in and out of sight between olive trees, cypresses, and palms. While listening to the horses' rhythmic pace, Ray put his arm around me and, holding me close to him, murmured: "I want you close to me like this forever and ever." I shivered. In that one instant the enormous difficulties ahead of us flashed before me. "Do not fear," he added, "from now on we shall be together as we are now."

Together. That was it. Genova 1954 was the feeling and the promise that we would live together forever.

The day after Portofino, at 11 a.m., I boarded a train for Florence. An hour later, Ray left for Beaulieu. Hidden in a small drawer of my marquetry desk are the slides Ray took of Genova 1954, the paper napkin with the demonstration of the Pythagorean theorem, and a withered rose, the one in the picture on Ray's desk.

Together. In 1954 I crossed the Atlantic on a trip that sealed my future with Ray. Since then, Ray and I crossed the Atlantic together for over thirty years, building bridges between the old world and the new. Our first crossing together was in January 1958 on the Queen Elizabeth with one-year old Lavinia to spend a year in Europe beginning with six months in Paris. Our last crossing was to Warsaw in May 1989. Ray was so sick he could hardly stand. Yet he managed to shake hands with Lech Walesa while I was attending in Warsaw a conference on "Cicero in the State" organized by the Italian Foreign Minister Andreotti.

In Europe the Iron Curtain was falling. We witnessed its fall from the train while crossing the whole of Western Europe from Paris to Budapest, and then to Szeged, where Ray in the early 1930's had worked in functional analysis with Frigyes Riesz, and where he now had been invited to lecture, barely capable of standing on his feet. From Budapest we rode the Orient Express to Paris. Forced to stop in Torino, guests of Professor Ossola and his wife, Ray had to undergo a brief and painful procedure before reaching Paris where Claudia could not take care of us because her husband was in trouble. The publisher Antoine Gallimard took us in. From Paris we flew to New York. Paris, which had been the first "working station" for Ray and me a year after our marriage in 1958, became our last stop together on the old continent before his death. I was never to cross the Atlantic with Ray again.

Thirty-six years after Genova, on February 11, 1990, I walked Ray on Riverside Drive in New York. He leaned heavily on me. It was the day before Donatella, our youngest daughter's, 28th birthday. The air was mild. An early spring had started. It was Ray's last spring on earth. Less than a month later he vanished from this world in a golden sunset at home. Up to the last moment, he was weak but sensitive to everything around us.

***

We lived thirty-nine years close to one another, beginning with our meeting on Riverside Drive on December 8, 1951. As on that evening, on February 11, 1990, we sat on a bench. He told me, as he did on that December 8, 1951, that I was beautiful and that he loved me. I felt such a pang in my heart that I had to fight to hold back my tears. I kissed him on the forehead. I rebelled at the fact that our life together should become history.

We had married in March 1956 after two years of anguish in the dark and two years of fighting in the open. By standing always near me through thirty-nine years he had taught me how to fight to win as he had won in my class in 1951 when he fenced valiantly with Italian grammar and syntax. He said he was able to do it because he felt I was standing near him. We had two girls together, Lavinia and Donatella. Claudia lived with us, and his three children, Duncan, Ingrid, and Madeleine nearby with their mother. We tried to keep the family united as a new family. We learned together how to overcome physical and moral distances, to build bridges, to make our home a nest for the children, a shelter for friends, a meeting place for intellectual endeavors. Together we learned to think and to build. *"Pensare Insieme"* ("To think together") became the motto of our life.

In 1963, back East after a year of work in California, we bought one hundred acres of land in the Catskills. Within an immense forest, it contained six structures—one home to live in, a large Studium, a spring house, a workshop, a woodshed and a reservoir—a little, self-sufficient mountain home that Donatella called *La Casa della Neve* ("the House of the Snow"). On July 22, 1991, two friends, professors of classics, who visited us found the motto for our habitat: *"hic habitat felicitas."* July 22, Ray's birthday, had been a day of grand celebration for the family for the past thirty-nine years. *Felicitas* does not mean *happiness*. It means *good fortune:* "Good fortune lives here."

It was our togetherness, I guess, that brought us good fortune. At times it inspired us to try to turn bad luck into good or to stubbornly try to make what we wanted to have out of what we did not have. Most of the time we succeeded. Our household was never a home of blessed peace. Children quarreled and we quarreled, but we had peace in our hearts when at night in bed we held hands, planning together the next step for an enterprise dear to both of us. At the end of a long road and many crossings of the Atlantic Ocean, we built together the first existing "Italian Academy for Advanced Studies in America." I directed the restoration of the old Casa Italiana, chose its furniture and for three years kept alive a solid exchange of scholars across the Ocean. We built it, of course, firmly at Columbia which had been home to Ray for sixty-eight years. Before the Academy, we worked together to build the first bilingual-bicultural Italian-English school in New York, *la Scuola New York*, a bridge between Italy and New York. Neither *Academy* nor *Scuola* had found a proper building as yet when Ray died. The four years of my Directorship were spent in scholarly meetings to discuss political, historical, and literary issues. Most of my attention was dedicated at first to the creation itself of the building, a complicated task dealing with the alliance of a University with a foreign state, raising money for that scope over four years. I worked alone with the assistance of one student, Sue Yoo, a Korean young woman of exceptional ability who dedicated her four years as an undergraduate to helping me as a work-study while taking a full load of classes. Sue Yoo graduated the year of the inauguration of the Academy, moving on to a successful career as a lawyer.

Ray was in love with Italy. Instead of converting to Catholicism, in order to join me and the children on a common operational level, he converted to Italy. He spoke Italian like a native. Out of all of Europe he felt at home only in Italy. He was a British subject born of a British father living in Germany and of a Swiss-French mother, a Racine, who swore by the tragedian she called her "ancestor." Through many adventures, the family had reached America in two installments—the father in 1916, after more than a year of internment by the Germans, the mother and the three children in 1917, crossing the Atlantic on a French vessel during the submarine blockade.

Ray's and my coming to America as a consequence of wars on European territory gave us both the chance to compare notes on the symbolic function of the Atlantic Ocean in the building of our families. I used to state that Ray came at age ten with his mother, a helpless victim of World War I, while I came by an act of free will after World War II, the wife of a liberator of Europe who could have chosen to stay in Europe *ad infinitum* (or what looked like that in 1945 in the wake of Yalta). I had told my first husband Claude, however, that I preferred to face life in the New World rather than to have the Americans dominate Europe. Ray and I had endless discussions on the subject.

It was perhaps in consequence of these discussions that I resorted to writing about our relationship to Europe, to America, and to what lay in between. When I sat at my Olivetti typewriter nobody could question my story. Fighting with words became then a pleasant chore if not an escape. Michael, Lavinia's eternal boyfriend before they married in the spring of 1990, used to say: "when she dies, we'll bury her with her 1945 Olivetti."

Ray, through secret channels, taught me virtues that I could not have learned otherwise. Only through love could I learn patience, humility, and faith in myself. How this learning was perfected through the years, it is impossible to tell. Two years after his physical death I can say he taught me what life is at its best. He used to say I taught him how to live. While Ray made me aware of the substance that makes for life; I offered him a way of *living it.*

In the bitter loneliness that I experience now because of his physical absence, when from the murky waters of memory little islands emerge, *brandelli di vita vissuta insieme* ("slivers of a shared life"), and I find myself unable to piece them together, in order to overcome the inexorable, I fumble through diaries and the five hundred and seventy letters saved in a big box in the country which we read on special occasions to the children.

In the summer of 1986, as we discovered the seriousness of Ray's illness, an entire world emerged from our letters of 1952-53, from the tons of words that had only apparently been drowned under the heavy sheets of life lived as a family—husband, wife, and children of different marriages, along with children of the children. Leafing through those letters felt like cleaning out our spring in the forest after a drought, when the reservoir tells us that water is becoming scarce. Actually, the water is still there. Only deeper down.

What Ray and I discovered together with our children was simply that we still had within ourselves that powerful urge to live that brought us, in 1956, to join our lives in marriage. A few weeks after rereading our letters from the early '50's, I left alone for my last sabbatical—two months in Europe—, motivated I don't know by what mean, masochistic instincts. I never suffered a more severe case of love-sickness than I did during those two months of planes, trains, buses, libraries, congresses, and meetings. I saw Ray everywhere and longed to touch him, to feel him, alive, next to me. The miracle took place during that particular separation. Ray wrote to me every day, pouring out his love for me. Marvelous letters that fully answered in great depth those I had written to him in 1952-53 while he was in Europe with his family, and to which he had answered only briefly.

In 1986, Ray began his final painful ordeal. At times very ill, the writing of those letters helped him forget his pain and look at life with a smile. The family gave him the will to fight his illness. He actually got better. By the time I returned, he could hold me in his arms without shaking. Of course, the girls at home—our daughters and Lucia—had been close to him and had made it possible for him to physically survive. Had it not been for me, however, he said, this time he would have lost in the struggle to live. He lived four more years of quiet, intense happiness at home in New York and Napanoch, feeding my own active life, and never, ever allowing me to stop living as he had wanted me to live with all the energy and creativity of which I was capable.

First Steps Forward

I never dreamt of wilderness in the overpopulated Italy I lived in before I came to America—neither in Merano before the War nor during the War in a besieged Rome nor immediately following the War in subalpine *Zone A* of the *Venezia Giulia*. It was Manhattan, which, while still in Italy, I had chosen as the only place I wanted to live in in America, but which, under harsh, unexpected circumstances had made me desperately dream of 'wilderness.'

Wilderness is concretely defined by the choice of the property we bought in the Catskills after an intuitive Irish agent had shepherded us to see several others. It is guaranteed by the location of the property, belonging as it does to the Roundout Reservoir area, by its history and by the very fact that, in spite of a magnificent view advertised in the real estate announcement, the property we bought had not attracted any buyer for the three years it had been for sale.

The origin of what is now Yagerville Road where our property is located leads to a family of Yagers whose name appears on many gravestones of the cemetery where Ray, our children's nanny Lucia, my sister Bona and her husband Eddie lie today. A village called Yagerville grew up in the early nineteenth century as a cluster of farmhouses scattered along a road that cut through the forest, a road that zigzagged up East Mountain. It was built around a tannery that used the bark of hemlocks indigenous to this particular area of the Catskills. With the demise of the tannery, silence fell over the area. What remains of the old village is the cemetery which today's

81

"community," scattered on both sides of the Rondout Reservoir, treasures—a stunning collection of pre-civil war graves mixed in with yesterday's dead. When Ray died, Lavinia bought a piece of precious land near them for the entire family.

The Napanoch Wilderness for us defines itself through the effect it had on our family from 1963 to Ray's death in 1990. Difficult to describe if not through family history, the Napanoch wilderness challenged Ray and me for thirty years in moments of euphoria and comforted us in moments of despair.

A first challenge to our building a new life together had come up shortly after our marriage, in 1957, when Ray accepted an invitation from the Collège de France in Paris and the Accademia dei Lincei in Rome. Our first daughter, Lavinia, was hardly one year old when we dragged her along with ten-year-old Claudia (Ray's three children Duncan, Ingrid, and Madeleine joining us for the summer) to participate in the life of a 1958 'Europe' to whose intellectual resurrection in the after-War period Ray contributed a mathematical *tour de force* from Scotland to Sicily. Our 'rediscovery of Europe' was followed by two peaceful summers of intense academic work in solitary farms in the Northeast. We finally spent a year in California, as Ray taught at Stanford and I was invited to teach in an exceptionally rich and up-to-date Italian Department at Berkeley.

Berkeley had surfaced in our lives indirectly, as Ray and I were crossing the Atlantic in June 1960 on the Italian ship *Cristoforo Colombo*. We were on a *voyage de plaisir* to explore a pearl of the Mediterranean, Vettica di Mare, a town on the Amalfi coast perched like an eagle over the water. My brother's wife, Maria, and her brother Antonio Amato, head of the Interpol in Naples, both from Amalfi, had found an eighteenth-century villa for us from which we could enjoy the view of the sea and reach the water through one hundred and fifty steps carved out of the rock.

Nestled in a vast orchard of oranges, peaches, apricots, and plums, the villa offered a two-floor sequence of ample rooms where, among antique furniture, wax madonnas and saints set on paper flowers peered at us through glass enclaves. The old kitchen with an old-fashioned woodstove led me back to my adolescence. An ancient well was used in lieu of a refrigerator. A wide terrace overlooked the constantly blue sea with which Ray and I dialogued poetically at night under a star-studded sky.

Every day we climbed down to the sea, Ray carrying three-year-old Lavinia on his shoulders, and we savored the fruit from the trees warmed by the sun. By car, through the narrow, winding *costiera,* we explored, at our own risk, Amalfi, Ravello, Pompei, Ercolano, and Vietri where we chose hand-made, 'imperfect,' dishes which I still enjoy today.

Vietri was also at the time home to the former director of the Casa Italiana at Columbia, Giuseppe Prezzolini, much talked about in Italy. We were to catch up with Prezzolini ten years later on the sleepy lake of Lugano in Switzerland. The Casa Italiana of Columbia University at the time, however, was of no interest to us except for its theatre of which I had been named Director in 1952 shortly after I had left the College of St. Elizabeth in New Jersey.

With Vettica in store for us, never did I enjoy an Atlantic crossing as I did the one in 1960 on the *Cristoforo Colombo*. That crossing turned out to be an important moment for my future academic activities.

On a blue morning in the middle of the Ocean, I was sipping my broth close to the swimming pool, looking leisurely at our girls jumping in and out of the water like dolphins. Two colleagues in Medieval and Renaissance Studies, Ferdinando Maurino and Charles Trinkaus, who usually sunned themselves near me in semi-silence, raised the possibility of my chairmanship of the "Italian Medieval and Renaissance" section of the Modern Language Association of America. If I was open to the idea, they would strongly support by candidacy. *Condicio sine qua non* was, of course, my attending the forthcoming MLA meeting. The offer did not impress me at all. I did not know that the MLA was the powerful Modern Language Association of America nor what that Chairmanship meant. Even had I known, at that moment of my life I didn't care. I was perfectly happy with my new family and with my work at Barnard where I had contributed to the fusion of the Barnard and the Columbia Departments of Italian.

When they told me that the MLA meeting would take place the week after Christmas, I answered without hesitation, actually with relief: "Impossible. Ray and I dedicate Christmas week to the children. It is a family rule." The two smiled ironically and asked me to think it over. At night, in our berths, the children asleep, I casually informed Ray of the proposal. His *yes* hit me as bluntly as my *no* had hit my colleagues that morning: "Of course you accept," Ray stated with a smile. "You must accept. I will accompany you personally to Chicago at the next MLA meeting. Lucia will take care of the children." The next morning, at the pool, my change of mind pleased my colleagues. As for me, I soon forgot about both the offer and the MLA. My mind and soul were set on Vettica.

In our voyage to Vettica, Ray navigated in his ancient Austin through Portugal, Spain, Southern France, Northern and Coastal Italy, at 20 miles an hour, the speed he wisely judged safe for what was left of Europe's ancient roads after the Allied bombardments.

We puffed happily along during that first family voyage in old Europe, on what are now secondary roads, the two girls, Claudia and Lavinia, laughing and fighting in the back of the car. We stopped to enjoy stunning cities and villages and to savor the excellent local food, although it rarely agreed with Ray. We spent the nights in small, quaint inns, jewels of a past now surviving only in old postcards. In Cordova, two-year-old Lavinia suddenly woke up at night with horribly swollen lips. Three old doctors, called by Ray in emergency from the nearby hospital, stood around the crib for a long time, in thoughtful and solemn in silence, like the wise old doctors of Pinocchio, finally declaring the swelling due to a spider bite.

While we were slowly winding our way down to the Amalfi Coast, Charles Trinkaus informed us that after we had disembarked, he had saved our desolate nanny Lucia from sunstroke. At the time this seemed to be a more significant event than the MLA meeting.

The 1960 MLA meeting in Chicago on the week after Christmas was for me a *veni vidi vici* moment like Caesar's conquest of Gaul. Not only was I elected Chairman of the MLA Italian Renaissance Section, but I was invited for a year as Visiting Professor at Berkeley. Ray without difficulty would commute from Stanford to Berkeley. We accepted the offer for January 1963. Our second daughter Donatella, born on February 12, 1962, celebrated her first birthday in Berkeley.

That is how, during our first married years, Ray and I led our horses side by side through the forest of life—like the Wandering Knights of the Renaissance, Christians and Muslims alike, Orlando and Agricane in pursuit of their beloved Angelica. In those years, I was passionately introducing my students as well as my children, to the chivalric poems of the Italian Renaissance: *The Cavalieri Erranti* or wandering knights. Those knights would casually stop at a given clearing and act out a new episode per Canto in the poem of their lives.

Napanoch suddenly emerged as a new Canto in our lives. A true milestone in the development of our relationship, it had come about in 1963 unexpectedly, as a cry of revolt, the expression of my sudden longing for a freedom that only a house in the wilderness could have given me.

It was October 1963, at 838 Riverside, on the Upper Drive between Broadway and the "real" Drive, in the apartment we had moved into near my sister Bona, after our marriage in 1956. The Upper Drive at 157th Street was deemed at the time sufficiently distant from the Columbia campus as to allow some lingering gossip about us, me in particular, to dissipate, but it was still close enough to the Columbia campus to allow me to keep a vigilant eye on the family at home. By October 1963, we had been happily living there for seven years. Only the Columbia Riots in 1968 would drive us down to 116th Street and Riverside Drive. More precisely to 445 Riverside where I still live today.

Shortly after our return from California, on an evening in early October 1963, Ray and I were alone in the living room that we had furnished with antique European furniture. Ray was lying on the sofa, eyes closed as usual, dreaming of a theorem, while I, sitting at my seventeenth century Dutch marquetry desk, was stubbornly and unsuccessfully trying to solve a difficult exegetical problem of manuscript discordance in the Latin critical edition of a Renaissance humanist. Both Ray and I were very much aware that my tenure at Barnard hinged on my contract for its publication by a prestigious Italian publisher. My deadline was 1965.

Claudia, Lavinia, and Donatella were asleep. That day had been for me a mixture of activities, an elegant swinging 'à la Tarzan' from tree to tree without falling, as one of my students years later was to describe my teaching style in a course evaluation. It had been an intense day like many others, finally ebbing towards a quiet evening of personal work when, for no apparent reason, I suddenly burst out complaining that things could not go on like this. In order to get to my real work beyond courses, meetings, children and other activities, I declared on the verge of tears, I needed to isolate myself. Ray opened his eyes and looked at me quizzically. This just incentivized me to continue.

"Yes, I know what I personally need at this point in my life," I burst out in despair, "I need a house in the wilderness where I can withdraw with you and the children and Lucia… a house where we can be by ourselves… away from this world of apartments and playgrounds, these *"parchetti,"* a little house in a forest… perhaps near a river, where we could escape on weekends… wake up with the sun as I did as a child." The *parchetto* was the "small children's playground" of the Upper Drive where I regularly spent part of my afternoons overseeing the children instead of working at my personal research project. Lucia and I both hated it. Ray got up from the sofa and without a word led me, as one does a child, away from my desk. In bed we fell asleep, holding hands as usual.

My outburst took place a few months after we had returned to New York from our stay in Berkeley, having crossed the continent by car. Though we had both agreed not to accept an advantageous offer for me to transfer from Columbia to Berkeley because we wanted to raise our girls in New York, the Berkeley experience had marked our conquest of America, as our land of adoption. Ray had supported me in Berkeley with the same fierce enthusiasm with which I had supported him on his mathematical tour of Europe at the end of our stay in 1958. We were by now ready to move on towards our next adventure on even terms.

In October 1963, there was no apparent reason for me to despair. By the time we had returned to the Columbia campus we were consciously proud of our marriage in which family and academic life were peacefully and constructively interwoven in a togetherness founded on inner happiness. Yet, the year in Berkeley had allowed me to taste a newer kind of freedom as a woman, a sense of personal freedom that had first caught me by surprise upon my arrival at Barnard in the fall of 1951. Upon my return to New York in 1963, I suddenly felt it would take me years of intense personal effort to reconquer that freedom on the Columbia campus because of my marriage to Ray.

Why 'my marriage to Ray?' everybody around me at that time would have asked. In 1954, at the height of the relationship's crisis, I, the only tenureless member of the four colleagues involved in the scandal of our two recent divorces, risked losing my job as I was being accused of having caused Ray's divorce. Millicent McIntosh and Thomas Peardon, Dean of the College and Dean of the Faculty respectively, had bravely and convincingly defended my case. Subsequently, in an unforgettable personal meeting, McIntosh had asked me to move on with my life at Barnard, undaunted by the accusation, acting precisely as I had acted thus far. Millicent had great faith in me, she told me, as a teacher and scholar who could combine the two with motherhood. Deeply touched by her words, I followed her advice and had given Barnard all of myself during the previous nine years. Proud of the freedom I enjoyed in my work at Barnard, as early as 1953 I had crossed Broadway and joined the Columbia Italian Department at the Casa Italiana, as the most natural thing to do. So far, I had obtained all I had longed for. At about the same time, I had joined Paul Oskar Kristeller in his indefatigable work of rediscovery of Renaissance Humanistic texts, working on Aristophanes and Apollonius of Rhodes.

What surfaced suddenly that night at 838 Riverside Drive was not the frustration I had repeatedly expressed as a woman between 1952 and 1954 when I had fallen under the spell of an adoring yet unreachable Ray. In October 1963, my outburst came out of sheer physical exhaustion. It was also in part the sudden outburst of a frustrated academic who, in a moment of exhaustion from the family chores added to her academic duties, had no more energy left for her 'real work.' That work had to be done. I had stubbornly stuck to it during the years of the War in Europe and my first American years, and after 1955, with Ray's constant indispensable support. It may have also perhaps been something more, at least as Ray perceived it. The firm will to succeed as a woman, mother, and scholar at the same time.

Only Ray could understand my outburst. He knew I needed recognition and respect for my scholarly work. I had to complete the critical edition of Valla's *De Voluptate* whose manuscripts I was consulting in the rare books collection of Columbia's Butler Library. A House in the Wilderness was a place where I could be fully myself in both my love for Ray and our children and in my own personal work which I had desperately pursued so far in my rare moments of freedom. That outburst eight years after our marriage was a call for another adventure together, this time a permanent one like our marriage or the birth of our daughters.

A few days later at the dinner table, in front of the girls and Lucia, he handed me an elegantly bound catalogue entitled *Farms from Ocean to Ocean*. As I was drifting from farm to farm, encouraged by the wealth of the offers, from Arizona or Alabama to Idaho, Montana and the Great Lakes, he gently intervened with the request that I not dream in the void. I should choose a place at one hundred miles distance from the Columbia campus, in the Catskills perhaps, he added ironically, where he used to ski on weekends with his former wife when she was still a young girl fresh from Norway. Memories of his previous marriage surfaced rarely in our life, always in a deeply ironical context. That was how Ray expressed his hostility against his ex-wife, a hostility which fortunately decreased with the years, perhaps in part with the help of Napanoch.

A House in the Wilderness

Ray and I bought the 'properties,' the houses, and most of the mountain called East Mountain on which they stand seven years after our marriage, in 1963. It happened on the day of Kennedy's assassination, on November 22, 1963. We discovered what had just happened in Texas at a toll station on route 17 while on our way to our future home. The events stunned both us and the lady lawyer, owner of the property, so much so that we mechanically and absent-mindedly went through what should have been for Ray and myself a most memorable process.

All I remember of that day was that it rained heavily in a most depressing manner while Ms. Severn opened Uncle Oscar's house to us and made it ours by serving us tea and homemade cookies on his old cups and dishes, some of which are still in use today. Some form of relief came only at dinner, a huge steak and a bottle of Frascati wine, in a warm restaurant in the valley at the foot of the mountains, in historic Napanoch. While we ate and mostly drank, we were entertained by Louise Severn with stories of the Village of Napanoch, fifteen miles away from 'our property' along the Rondout Creek. The Village was founded, like the well-known village of New Paltz in the valley of the Hudson, by the Huguenots, a French Protestant sect, ancestors of Ray's French / Swiss mother, Marthe Racine.

Three huge "Family Books," like the manuscript tomes on which I spent my best hours of the War at the Vatican Library, now document how our *House in the Wilderness* became, through the years, the home of our family of women with Ray as our center and leader. A home where we laughed and cried together, worked side by side and played, all our quarrels ending sooner or later in reconciliation. By when, late that November night in 1963, we reported the acquisition of the house to the family on the Upper Riverside Drive in New York, the house in the wilderness had already become a page in our personal book of American History.

We owe our Village in the Catskills to the careful, step-by-step, creative art of Oscar Ullmann, a Viennese violinist stockbroker who, in his mid-fifties, in the early 1930's, left Wall Street and diligently explored the whole East coast for a little corner of land where he could build his American home. I was at that time an adolescent happily reading Homer and Horace in a little town in the Alps. Ray had just married his Norwegian young lady. Uncle Oscar, as his nieces called him, finally bought from the local Osterhoudt family, which had owned the land since the Civil War, one hundred acres on East Mountain, in the foothills of the Catskills, above what was to become the Rondout Reservoir. In fact, the Reservoir was being built at that very time as part of the vast Water Reserve of New York City.

Midway to the top of East Mountain, Oscar Ullmann had excavated a terrace wide enough to make room for what was to become his little white alpine village. It must have vaguely reminded him of those villages he had left behind in his beloved Austria—a two story house, a spring house, a workshop, a three car garage for his WWII weapons carrier, a woodshed and a cement reservoir up the mountain to collect the water of the spring that once upon a time had made the place habitable for some Dutch settlers. The water of the spring reaches the house through copper pipes via the so-called springhouse. There it is kept running into a cement bathtub throughout the year so that it will not freeze in the harsh winters when temperatures can reach below zero and so that the copper does not accumulate in the drinking water. A path in the forest up the mountain leads to an orchard rich in knarled apple trees. Even before entering the house on my first visit, I fell in love with the apple orchard, seeing all those trees loaded with red and yellow apples ready to be picked. In the meanwhile, Ray, who was diligently exploring the house with the agent, had fallen in love with its stout stone-walled cellar. For both of us it was love at first sight. That is what I told the two Miss Severn, heirs to the property, when I visited them in New York.

After having carved his name, like the author of a book, on a corner stone of the foundation, Ullmann left New York City for good and became a citizen of Napanoch, the closest village to Yagerville Road, to which he commuted by weapons carrier. His picture in our living room reminds us constantly of all that we owe him. He died at 83, having completed his village, the cellar and the ground floor of the main house. He left us to complete the upper floor and to add, over the years, a pond and a barn among many other improvements.

Volume I of our three Family Books opens with a picture of Ullmann playing the violin alongside Einstein. His home— kitchen, large living room, three bedrooms and one ample bathroom—had become the meeting place of German refugee musicians and intellectuals.

On November 22, 1963, Ullmann's niece, a stout, middle-aged lady of sober, old-fashion elegance, handed us the keys of the house, just as Uncle Oscar had left it. With the house came furniture and dishes, the Austrian horsehair mattresses with linens, the armchair where he used to rest after a day of hard work near the huge stone fireplace, in the middle of a rustic yet elegant living room under worn out beams, surviving remnants of dead neighboring farms.

Ms. Louise Severn and her sister, an actress who had played alongside Eva LaGallienne, loved animals, and they housed over twenty cats in their Madison Avenue apartment. Although they loved cats, they did not love the wilderness in which uncle Oscar had retired, the property that had been advertised as the "house with a million-dollar view" and that had remained on the market for three years. It was perhaps waiting for us, unconscious lovers of the 'wilderness.' Ray and I had to swear we did not hunt. Ray, not I, could even boast of loving cats. Yet Ray and the real estate agent agreed that what had finally made the sisters consent to sell after a month of hesitation—and to even lower the price—was my own personal visit to the home of their cats on Madison Avenue. There I had shared the story of my own childhood in the Alps of the Süd-Tirol and of Ray's birth and childhood in the Swiss Jura, the whole spiced with a touch of our love story.

Two-year-old Donatella, fresh from our year in California, baptized our Catskillian village "*La Casa della Neve*," or "The

House of Snow," the magic place of stories I told her in bed at night. We all agreed that what Oscar's Alpine Village missed was a church with a steeple. Instead of a church, Michael, Lavinia's husband and lover of animals, like his children, more than half a century after Ray and I bought the place built a state-of-the art barn that houses alpacas, llamas, goats, a donkey called Lucy, some chickens, numerous peacocks, and two cats. 'Napanoch' remains today the home of the family that Ray and I conceived of when we dangerously sailed through two divorces, risking if not our lives at least my career at Barnard/Columbia, which, in 1954, implied my whole life in America.

Beyond actual facts, it is the very nature of our personal relationship after our marriage that unconsciously led us to conceive of a physical place within which human dissent dissolved into peace and constructiveness. A naïve, ambitious ideal which we would have made fun of had we openly confessed it to ourselves as such. We came to it gradually.

Between 1970 and 1990, our Napanoch/Yagerville wilderness increasingly became the meeting point of all those among our friends in New York and Western Europe who believed in the unification of Western with Eastern Europe and who worked towards it.

***

Napanoch came into being as the latest in a chain of events set in motion by our marriage in 1956. We had rediscovered our Europe together in 1958 with our first crossing of the Ocean with the new family. Our year in Berkeley in 1963 stands today as our first discovery of America beyond the Hudson. Berkeley in itself and my first crossing of the continent by train and car meant the conquest of those 'open spaces' I had dreamt of since 1947-48 as a young war bride living with my then husband Claude, my sister Bona and baby Claudia in a modest apartment on 181st Street and Bennett Avenue. In 1948, on a boat trip from New York to

Schenectady, I remember that I burst out in joy imagining the land beyond the Hudson. These were moments of joy that I treasured in my four years of life with Claude in America. We divorced in 1955.

With our marriage Ray and I embarked on a voyage in which "the folly of love" as life's basic creative impulse led us like wandering knights from clearing to clearing, acting out our love in its many expressions from Catullus' *"Da mihi basia mille et deinde centum, Lesbia"* ("Give me a thousand kisses, Lesbia, followed by another hundred") to some new unexpected adventures across the Atlantic Ocean. What spurred us on was the concrete force of our togetherness.

Too many meetings, connections, courses, congresses, projects of all kinds, too many to mention in order of time and space. I often think of our last meeting with Italo Calvino at his house in Rome in June of 1985 when Ray and I were living with excitement the last steps of a chain of adventures whose final success, the creation of the Italian Academy of Advanced Studies in America, Ray would not live to enjoy.

We met in Rome, the four of us—Calvino and his wife, Ray and myself. Calvino died a few months after our visit, shortly before delivering his lectures at Harvard which he was preparing when we visited him. He died of a sudden death like many of the knights of the chivalric poems he loved. Darkness fell upon him, a sunset at midday, as he was acting out one of his "adventures" in the clearing of the forest of his life. His death shocked me as a dark cloud that suddenly obscures the sun, foreshadowing death near me.

During our meeting we had spoken of *errare* and *esistere,* of wandering and existing, and of the knights of the Italian Renaissance who existed in their ceaseless wandering through the miracle of their quest for love, oblivious of the noble Cause of God and Country which had made them famous in the Medieval French epic.

"Com'e' che fate a prestar servizio se non ci siete?" "How can you engage in combat if you don't exist?" asks the French emperor Charles to Agilulfo, the *Cavaliere Inesistente,* the Inexistent Knight in Calvino's homonymous novel. The knight answers that what spurs him on is 'the cause' of God and Country.

"E' già ben ditto che si fa il proprio dovere... Per uno che non esiste siete proprio in gamba." "Very well said. That's the way one carries out one's duty. You are really sturdy for someone who doesn't exist," concludes the wise Emperor as he moves on matter of factly, like a general at any time and any place.

Calvino, Ray, and I spoke of the *esile filo,* the thin thread that ties the 'existent' to the 'non-existent'. We spoke of mathematics and poetry and of a school for his daughter in New York. He would have liked her to continue her studies in America. Calvino and I had planned to offer a course together at Barnard and Columbia on Ariosto's *Orlando Furioso,* "Orlando's Fury," to which I had added Boiardo's *Orlando Innamorato* or "Orlando in love." I taught that course with the philosopher Ernesto Grassi shortly before Ray's death.

I tried hard recently to remember details of our conversation. All I could grasp was a general feeling of lightness tinged with gentle melancholy, as when Agilulfo, the non-existent knight, plays at night with pinecones to build triangles. There is lightness and anguish in his playful mood.

We met Calvino in 1985. By 1985, at Barnard and Columbia life triumphed around us, sending powerful waves of new energy to our refuge in the wilderness. By June 1986, "Medieval and Renaissance Text and Studies" at the State University of Binghamton had published the course I had given at Barnard with Ernesto Grassi, "Folly and Insanity in Renaissance

Literature," which explored the thin thread that separates the folly (of love) from insanity in poetic creation.

Old Ernesto had become by then a member of the Napanoch family, the *"gamba rotta-mangia minestra"* ("Broken-leg Soup-eater") as he had baptized himself for old Lucia. He shared with us Napanoch and Ischia just as Giuseppe Sansone had shared Napanoch and Capri with us at the onset of Ray's and my long voyage together through life; as Armand Bérard and his family had shared Paris and the Pyrenees; and between 1986 and 1991 how with the Italian consul in New York, the unforgettable Ministro Francesco Corrias, we had shared Rome's old heart and mind and Napanoch's creative wilderness.

Between 1986 and 1989 Napanoch had built a reputation as the center of a shared joint life. First in a long chain, Vittore Branca and his family had for many years shared Napanoch with Venice, Carlo Ossola had shared Napanoch withTorino. The critical edition of Valla's *De voluptate*, Napanoch's first natural child, had been nursed by the philosopher Paul Kristeller, a German refugee from Berlin who had fortuitously been a guest of Oscar Ullmann. A dialogue Napanoch/München via New York had given birth in München to *A Defense of Life: a Renaissance Theory of Pleasure*, the main offspring of the critical edition at which I was working desperately in October 1963 when we decided to buy a House in the Wilderness. Ullmann's garage which had been turned by us into a *Studium*, as Kristeller had baptized it in 1969, to host Claudia's engagement party with the Parisian Bernard, had become by then the family workshop and the meeting place for heated discussions with guests from overseas.

By 1989 Napanoch, together with our apartment at 445 Riverside Drive, had turned into a point of convergence of Italian, French, German, British, Polish, Hungarian, and Russian "wandering knights" looking for adventures with their American counterparts. In Napanoch, in the Studium or by a roaring fire under the towering pines of the terrace, a family of Europeans and Americans enjoying Lucia's lasagne, was yearning for a peaceful dialogue between a divided Europe and a much-admired America.

By Ray's death in March 1990, the end of the Cold War that Ray and I had witnessed in Warsaw, Budapest, and Vienna in late 1989 led us to bring our Napanoch quietly back to what it was meant to be when Ray and I had originally set eyes on it in October 1963. It was the natural *locus* for a peaceful life within the family and the meeting point of our children and grandchildren scattered through a world that would have been unimaginable during the thirty years of the Cold War. This happened through the rite of Christmas.

As Ray was dying in 1990, he and I felt that Napanoch had to remain what it had always been for us—a peaceful workshop where we experienced the pleasure of being ourselves in a form of freedom that seeks genuine togetherness as the world around us changes and we ourselves change with it.

Twenty years after Ray's death, the family that Lavinia has stubbornly kept on the Columbia campus drives me every weekend 102 miles north along the Hudson, the distance Ray had chosen in 1963 for our house in the wilderness, now the point of convergence of a family that is scattered throughout the world. We know that Ray waits for us, resting in the old rural cemetery at the base of Yagerville Road. There he lies peacefully with old Lucia, Eddie, and Bona surrounded by the many Yagers—among them even a Lavinia. Yagerville Road was still unpaved when Ray and I took over Ullmann's little village in 1963.

At the distance of years from Ray's physical disappearance, I see the sequence of events that created our home as an expression of the positive 'folly of love,' of love as life's basic creative force which, as one grows older and more involved with life, assumes, beginning with its earliest stage, different expressions without diminishing in intensity. The creative expressions of our love, our family and academic life, were all interconnected.

At difference from Uncle Oscar, Ray and I never thought of giving up New York City and Columbia because they constituted a means through which we could build a bridge to Europe across an Ocean that millions of Europeans like us had crossed before us. Napanoch offered us the possibility of sharing our life with our children, and when the world beyond Europe opened up to them, in spite of great distances, they would always join us in Napanoch for Christmas.

The Rite of Christmas

The rite of the Christmas Tree was celebrated in Napanoch every year by the whole family between the 21st and the 24th of December, culminating on the night of December 24 with a special ceremony centered on a lively *Bambino Gesù* ("Baby Jesus"). Inspired by a harmonious combination of the winter solstice and the Christian myth, the event had also signified for Ray and myself the union of the Old World with the New, the old Alpine myths of our childhood and the American wilderness we had recently acquired. In Europe, in fact, the villages where we were born—Ray fourteen years before me—and where we spent our childhood, both lay in the Central Alps, in the heart of Europe, at a short distance from one another as the crow flies. For me in particular, but also for Ray who was in love with the details of my childhood, there was the vivid memory of a special Christmas Tree, the first and the last Christmas Tree of my childhood.

It was the pungent aroma of an old fir, the Christmas tree of those early years of my life and of that space bigger than life, a *Tannenbaum* that reached the ceiling of papa's library in the heart of the Alps at the foot of the Dolomites. In my imagination, as a five-year-old, I identified my one-month-old sister Bona, whose crib appeared near the Christmas tree when I entered the room, with the newborn Baby Jesus. When the bell rang and the door of the library opened, all the wax candles were lit on the branches of the tree, their flames flickering off of shining ornaments of all shapes and colors. The whole room was flooded by the discreet fluttering lights of the miraculous tree, while out of the wide windows stretched a garden blanketed with snow. Beyond it rose the Dolomites, whose steep peaks the sun painted pink at sunset. Six months later my father died suddenly of a heart attack in that very library, on the armchair which had been removed to make room for the magic Christmas tree. After his death, in her superhuman effort to secure the family's survival, my mother, left bankrupt with four children to support, eliminated everything that was not essential to life. The rite of a magic tree at Christmas was not essential.

Ray's and my family's Christmas celebration, influenced by the medieval Christmas plays I had directed through the years with my Barnard students in the theater of the Casa Italiana, seemed to tacitly imply a kind of Aristotelian unity of place— our home in the wilderness of Napanoch's East Mountain as the *condicio sine qua non* of its performance. The choice of Napanoch as the irreplaceable Bethlehem of our celebration had never been questioned as long as Ray lived. He had always been the director of our Christmas "performance." After 1980, he had been assisted in this responsibility by Michael who, after Ray's death, took over the entire production. By Christmas 2009, Dony's four children, Madeline, Nicholas, Alexander, and Lucas, had participated enthusiastically in it for four years.

Our first Napanoch Christmas dates back to December 1963, two months after the acquisition of our property. Christmas was the first of two-yearly celebrations in our family life in Napanoch from 1963 to Ray's death. The other, the July 22 celebration of

Ray's birthday which took place in the heat of the summer, was sheer enjoyment for all of us as we presented, in homage to Ray, a series of art shows and plays that the children invented, making light of their parents' "manic obsession" with memories of their European past and their love of their American present. I remember the Parisian Bernard, Claudia's husband, playing a cow in Lamboing, Ray's childhood hamlet near Geneva, and Lodovico Branca, son of my friend and colleague Vittore Branca, playing the protagonist in *Ferdinand the Bull*, which mocks professional haughtiness and aggression. July 22, a feast of our own invention, stopped naturally with Ray's death in 1990 while the Christmas rite still lives on.

In 1963, opening our house to our neighbors, which we regularly did the day after Christmas in later years, would have been the direct American way to express our natural desire as newcomers to the mountain to connect with the world around us. But neighbors were difficult to find. We could have counted on one only neighbor, an old retired school teacher who lived alone on a big farm at the bottom of our road. We were both unaware when we had bought our wilderness that it was situated in a depressed area in the state of New York, hence very sparsely populated. The added recent expropriation of the whole verdant Rondout Valley by New York City for its water supply scattered our few surviving neighbors through the thickly wooded East Mountain, each at a considerable distance from one another and from us. Fortunately, most of them were looking for work. We met them through the years one by one, as we still meet them today, when we needed work done around the house and the property that neither of us could perform. Though both Ray and I enthusiastically read Laura Ingalls Wilder's Little House books to our daughters every night in front of a crackling fire, we were very different from the Pa or Ma of the story. The farm work we could perform was limited to what we nostalgically recalled from our childhood summers in the Alpine villages of our mothers, such as cutting the grass with a real scythe, raking it with a long wooden rake, loading it with a pitchfork onto the WWII weapons carrier inherited from Oscar Ullmann, and finally piling it in special spots of the forests for the hungry deer foraging for food in winter's snow.

The first guests to share with us the joy of Christmas in 1963 were the faithful and loyal members of my old European family: my sister Bona who had received Ray and me in her apartment in 1954 after our divorces and had even designed and sewn my Chinese wedding dress; her husband Eddie, German anti-Hitler hero who had recently completed his Ph.D. at Columbia in German and Russian nineteenth century esthethics; their children, Vico and Carlo, twins to our two daughters; and their nanny, the severe and matter-of-fact Fernanda who came from the town of Rovereto near our home town in the Alps. Although the house as we entered it, shortly before Christmas, had beds for only the six members of our immediate family, we invited the whole of Bona's clan to stay with us for the complete Christmas vacation: eleven in all. Sleeping wherever, we happily worked together to invent, realize, and enjoy our first 'American Christmas' in the wilderness.

Our 1963 Napanoch Christmas Play focused not on the boldly commercialized Santa Claus that surrounded us all over the U.S. but on the birth of a child—a special child born in a manger in a corner of Palestine at the climax of the Roman Empire, when the whole world seemed to have found peace. The center of our play was a baby Jesus not the historical Jesus featured in the gospels but more precisely the one drawn from within my childhood memory.

The little Baby Jesus was made in Italy like the rest of the characters of the manger by humble artists who had drawn the story of the Nativity not from the gospels but from the country's ancient popular theater. Our day-long Napanoch ceremony may also have been inspired by some medieval miracle plays that I had produced in the early 1950's in the Casa Italiana Theater.

Both Claudia and Lavinia had had their first stage experience as characters in one of those 'miracle plays' called *Il Miracolo del Pellegrino* ("The Pilgrim's Miracle"). By far my best 'Madonna' in those days was my student and assistant Joan Ferrante, later to marry Millicent McIntosh's son Carey and become Chairman of the Columbia English Department.

Whatever its source may have been, the play we improvised every Christmas in Napanoch from 1963 on, a marriage of popular medieval legend with the wilderness we loved, was meant to celebrate our personal feeling of achievement and joy after the acquisition of our lot of American wilderness. Inspired by my early childhood memory of intense light flooding from a huge evergreen, our Napanoch Christmas celebrated, through a historically and religiously famous birth, the triumph of light and life over darkness and death.

Our Christmas play required a whole day of hard work for both children and adults, as we organized it together in harmony and laughter, with a shared awe at the results, as if its success depended on our work being validated by the final miracle. On Christmas eve we got up early, in a house heated by a huge crackling fire in the very living room where the event was to take place. After breakfast, the adults led the children on a long walk through the forest up the mountain in a contest as to who would find the best tree, tall and robust enough to protect, under its wide green limbs, the increasingly large manger that we would build under it. We dragged the tree down to the house, cut it down to touch the ceiling and adorned it with trimmings inherited from my family in Europe. Electric lights had replaced the original candles of my childhood. The children then focused on the manger's backdrop, a sheet painted in intense blue and dotted with vivid stars and cotton cumulus clouds. The forest, ahead of the snowfall, had donated moss, rocks, pebbles, pinecones, acorns and contorted branches of green mountain laurel that served as trees. Angels, shepherds, sheep, and sheepdogs "from nearby villages" surrounded the holy family, with cows and oxen scattered throughout the mossy landscape. Baby Jesus, not yet born, was housed on the fireplace's mantle until the evening's final miracle.

At sunset, with everything in place, we gathered around Ray at the piano to practice the Christmas carols that each adult remembered in his native tongue. Finally, the door to the living room was locked and we all gathered, tired but happy, in a warm kitchen where Lucia by now had prepared the Christmas eve meal. Once the kitchen was cleaned up, all lights were turned off as we waited in the kitchen in silence, looking out at the night stars, trying to spot the one star that was to bring Baby Jesus into his manger along with the magical appearance of the gifts under the Christmas tree. The ringing of a bell in the living room was the sign that Baby Jesus had arrived: we then opened the living room door in awe to witness the magic of Christmas.

On that first Napanoch Christmas in 1963, two-year-old Dony with my help distributed the gifts one by one. She was the first the next morning to discover the stocking hanging from the fireplace— one for each child. In 1989 we celebrated the last Christmas in Ray's life with sixteen people of the extended family including Michael's parents, Isot who came from Bavaria, and Howard.

I remember the Christmas of 2008, the last of the many we had spent all together in Napanoch with the "cousins" from Washington before their departure for Africa. As our overloaded car on December 23 painfully climbs up Yagerville Road, an overexcited Tristan insists we should be there before the cousins. We barely make it in time to reach the house when we spot the cousins behind us. The children rush out and disappear into the forest. Hours later, a sky full of stars, they sit in a row, all six of them, their back to the window, on the bench at the long kitchen table. Lavinia, master of ceremonies and director of all household operations, reminds them that they must get up early tomorrow. The next morning, children and adults move to the forest for the ritual operation: the yearly search for the tree, the king of the forest. For a while they stomp in the snow, pointing, discussing, discarding, until Michael judges and decides. Michael takes out the saw. The tree is felled, its limbs softly bouncing off of the fresh snow. The children take turns in dragging it home where Michael and Dony's husband John cut it down to the requisite nine feet, allowing its tip to reach the ceiling and its robust arms to fill the corner of the living room.

The children give the last strokes to the backdrop of the manger. They set the hut up on a mound of moss, pinecones, and rocks. Palm trees and orange trees, the house plants, provide elevation and depth. Finally, the stage is set for the appearance of the characters of the "nativity play," an army of familiar statuettes, some showing clear signs of decay from decades of use. The three Kings on their camels are kept at a good distance, behind a rock, as usual, for they are to arrive at the hut only on the Epiphany, January 6.

With all the main characters in place, all except for Baby Jesus, a small cup of milk is set on the mantle of the fireplace for the overloaded donkey which, on that very evening, December 24, will drag a bag of gifts up the steep road. When all is in place, the children surround Lavinia at the piano to practice Christmas carols from the softly worn hymnals. After dinner, children and adults look intently out from the kitchen window at the night sky to identify the arrival of Baby Jesus. And, just as in past, at the ringing of a bell, the living room opens to display the much-expected miracle—the magical appearance of the gifts along with the statuette of Baby Jesus that has miraculously been placed amid the hay in the manger. One by one, the children tiptoe to the piano and sing the three Christmas hymns that would finally allow them to reach…. the end of the "play," the opening of the gifts. The youngest child, in 2008 four-year-old Lucas, with the help of his mother Donatella, distributes the gifts. The next morning, Lucas, like his mother in 1963, is the first to find the stocking hanging from the mantle.

An entry of every child in the "Family Book" on January 3, 2009, witnesses the happiness of having participated in the event. Do they still believe, or do they stubbornly want to believe? Belief holds them together in harmony.

Our rite of Christmas was a myth born out of Ray's and my desire to build a solid Euro-American family that throughout the years would withstand all pressures and temptations of disaggregation from the stress and time of outside forces. Over the years that ceremony had become for us a deeply felt prayer.

Bridging Language and Culture

Beyond our need for the wilderness, the other essential foundation for our children's education was the choice of the school in New York in which to enroll them. Here again it was a matter of chance. We owe to Claudia at age nine the school that matched the Napanoch wilderness from 1964 to today, as even Lavinia's children attended it before entering college.

When we went to Paris in 1958, we had decided to register Claudia in a well-known French private school, l'école Sevigné, where she would be taken care of as 'a special case.' In January 1958, after a long crossing of the Ocean and a whole day driving on icy roads from Le Havre to Paris in our small and overstuffed Austin, Ray, Claudia, one-year-old Lavinia, and myself landed late at night in a little Parisian Hotel, *L'Hôtel des Saints-Pères*, on the Seine not far from Ray's place of work, the *Collège de France*, there to stay until we could find an apartment.

The day after our arrival, an enthusiastic Claudia faced her new school. A week later, however, she decided to fall sick thus helping herself and the family out of a serious impasse. In the peaceful days that ensued, by following her in the daily homework sent to us from the school, I realized that what she needed was help with her French—to say the least. I thus tutored her day and night for the two weeks of her 'illness,' mainly reading to her French poetry and history, which she adored. Back in school, I easily obtained from La Directrice that Claudia be placed in a lower grade than the one to which she had originally been placed based on her height. After that switch, Claudia seemed to fly as happy as a bird from her nest—the *Hôtel des Saints-Pères* first, and later our rambling apartment at Rue de Ranelagh near the Bois de Boulogne.

I recall with pleasure, in the dark moments of my American life, the vision of a charming little girl in a white, hand-embroidered dress, gift of her aunt Francesca in Rome, standing among Ray's colleagues, the cream of French mathematicians, and their wives. The *salon* is in the heart of the splendidly restored, unfurnished apartment near the Bois de Boulogne, whose walls, covered with mirrors, make it shine in its bareness. It had been very hard for us to find an apartment.

The Spring of 1958 was, to say the least, an exciting time for Paris. It marked the end of the Algerian revolution and of the French Fourth Republic. We lived day by day in suspense, afraid, among other things, of losing our apartment until de Gaulle took over. After two months at the *Hôtel des Saints-Pères* not far from the *Collège de France*, we had miraculously obtained that recently restored and unfurnished apartment thanks to the *Alliance France-Amérique*. We had succeeded in retaining it notwithstanding pressures by some Communist leaders that were the result of repeated interventions with the *Bureau de Logement* by Monsieur Bataillon, *Recteur du Collège de France*. A miracle in the chaos of Paris.

On a clear Parisian day in May in 1958 we had a party for Ray's French colleagues in the Salon of the Mirrors of our empty apartment. Little Claudia, part of the entertainment, standing on a chair, her image reflected by the mirrors on the walls, recites for them in unaccented French poems by Baudelaire and Victor

Hugo and some charming excerpts from her history book on the *reines de France* (Queens of France) for whom she had developed a deep attraction.

How did this little American girl ever learn French so well, the guests inquired? It was indeed "the miracle of Paris." The following day Claudia received as a gift from one of the ladies a copy of *"Le petit prince"* with a dedication. *"A une petite Américaine qui aime les reines de France"* ("to a little American girl who loves the Queens of France").

Claudia's early entrée into what was to become her bilingual/bicultural world may explain not so much her marrying a young Frenchman—whom she later divorced—as much as her forty years as an English teacher in the Parisian lycées. She even designed a university course for the training of French teachers based on phonetics.

Back in New York in the Fall of 1958, a ten-year-old Claudia declared she wanted to continue her schooling in French. Claudia, who in her early years had been stubbornly monolingual, had suddenly and enthusiastically become trilingual. Italian, which she had refused to accept at age two when her grandmother came expressly from Rome to Paris to take care of her, now came to her easily after French. Ray, whose maternal language was French, was delighted by her choice of school in New York. Her father, Claude, didn't mind. He had claimed the French origin of his family name, Bové, whereas the rest of the family had opted for Bove.

Claudia's first year at the Lycée of New York was very hard. Ray and I tutored her assiduously. After that first hump, however, she sailed successfully through the Lycée for seven years, successfully graduating with a 'baccalauréat' at the Lycée Châteaubriand in Rome during Ray's and my sabbaticals in 1966. She passed her Bac with the highest grades with an essay on Voltaire whose work she had studied at age fourteen, in a course of French literature at University of California Berkeley. There was no *Lycée Français* in Berkeley so we had sent her to University of California Berkeley French classes instead.

Lavinia and Dony successfully followed in her footsteps. They all switched to the Lycée Français de New York after a couple of years in an American school, in their case the traditional Saint Hilda's and Saint Hugh's near Columbia. By the time they were ten years old Europe had become part of their world.

The French Lycée of New York was an old-fashioned European school. We loved it because it did not interfere with the family's concept of education, which we had actually never clearly defined. Limiting its task to promoting a classical European program through rigorous discipline and traditional studying habits, its core curriculum in the early 1960's seemed perfect for us as the foundation for future studies.

Every Friday afternoon Ray and I, our nanny Lucia in tow, packed our three girls with their books into our Ford station wagon, and drove them to Napanoch. Renouncing all 'parties' and other attractions of New York society, our daughters would divide their day between books and play in the fields and forests.

I still remember the old Lycée of Monsieur Maurice Galy, the Headmaster or President as he was called, as a family school where we, as parents, felt perhaps more at home than our children did. Maurice Galy, a short, stocky, vivacious historian from the Pyrenees, alongside his effervescent and elegant wife Paule, dominated the school. Paule would organize elegant dinners and parties for American friends and donors where the students, dressed in eighteenth century costumes, served elaborate meals. Grayson Kirk, then President of the Lycée's Board of Trustees as well as President of Columbia, approved of all of Galy's initiatives *in absentia*. Rightly so, because the Galy couple succeeded on their own in giving to the school the seriousness of a good *Parisian Lycée* with a vague aura *à la "Louis XIV"* which, at that time, attracted New York intellectuals, artists, journalists, writers, bankers, and independently wealthy parents who had traveled to Europe before the War. Poor Haitians attended as well, on scholarship, while high-ranking diplomats of French-speaking former colonies constituted a special group highly treasured by the administration because they acted as promoters of French culture in America. They appreciated not only the French curriculum but also the elegant atmosphere of the school which soon occupied three mansions on Fifth Avenue between 72nd and 96th street.

One day, called upon by Galy to arbitrate between francophone African diplomats and American intellectuals, I had my first diplomatic success. I convinced the eloquent Monsieur Aké, Ambassador of Côte d'Ivoire, to accept a proposal, strongly supported by my colleague Alan Mandelbaum from New York University, to add to the curriculum one weekly period of American history.

Dony, like Lavinia, became the product of our educational "routine"—the New York/Napanoch one as well as the particular one of the Lycée. Dony probably forgot that, as the baby of the pack, she did not like the Lycée discipline, and had bargained with me after one year of Greek to replace Greek with German. I then had to dedicate the two-hour weekly drive from Napanoch to New York to reading out loud to her the pamphlet called *"Die Taubheit von Beethoven"* ("Beethoven's Deafness"). It was during those "classes in the car" that I trained Lavinia as well to learn all of the conjugations of irregular Greek verbs by heart.

Equally as vibrant though richer in content and more elaborate in presentation, those classes still take place with Lavinia's children, the next generation of Lycée students. They serve as the bridge between New York and Napanoch, linking our life in the city to our life in the wilderness.

By the time Dony reluctantly reached the Lycée after a kindergarten in Ankara and three years at Saint Hilda's & St. Hugh's we had transformed the three-car garage in Napanoch into a library and Art Hall—baptized *Studium* by the philosopher Paul Kristeller and his wife Edith who were among our first guests. From out of the swamp below the house we had also excavated a deep, perfectly round pond where we could swim in the summer and skate in the winter. Mamma who had visited us a couple of times from Rome greeted both with enthusiasm. She wove garlands of mountain laurel for the new Studium for the celebration of Claudia's engagement in 1969 and sat for hours watching the genesis of our pond as the many natural springs that make the wealth of our mountain fed it. For Mamma, born in a tiny village in an alpine valley, our 'Napanoch' was a miracle of the New World worthy of being quoted in the World Atlas.

The magic of Napanoch as it revealed itself after Ray and I had acquired the mountain hit both of us in a different way, causing us at first a moment of surprise as if we had suddenly discovered we were not made from the same mold.

"My nervous system is made of sticks," Ray in his twenties had written to John von Neumann in a note to explain why he would not accept the offer of an assistantship the already famous mathematician had extended to him. Many years later that nervous system reacted violently to the impenetrable forests that suddenly surrounded him. Ray, the King of Napanoch, simply refused to enter the 'Unknown' for fear of getting lost. It took him a few years to agree to follow me, marking the path with orange surveyor tape. I had to wait until Lavinia and Dony grew old enough to accompany me in my exploration of the forest. Until then I explored alone.

Each of the three daughters who had shared with us our adventurous life between New York, Napanoch, and Europe contributed as grown up women a world of their own, each one in her own continent. For Claudia it was Europe; for Lavinia, America—New York and Napanoch; for Dony... the world beyond the Mediterranean: China, the Himalayas, Pakistan, Afghanistan, Iraq, Africa, Nepal, Turkey—always reporting on wars, refugees, and natural disasters.

PART III—SPREADING OUT INTO THE WORLD

The passage of time from 1963 to the new millenium and the branching out of the family in separate units posed an obvious obstacle to unity of place. In 1994 Dony lured the Napanoch family to Africa where she was the New York Times East Africa Bureau Chief. Africa was to play an important role in future family experiences, and our little house in the wilderness would have to find its place in the larger world in which our daughters were living. Times had changed, and so had our own little nuclear family.

As a child Dony had been in love with myths. The "wandering knights" of the mythical Renaissance novels she loved had the whole world at their disposal—Europe, Asia, the island of a mysterious Atlantic Ocean, even the moon. And Dony dreamt of a mysterious world beyond Europe. Even so, in all her years of 'wandering,' Dony had missed Christmas in Napanoch only once.

By November 2009, times had changed dramatically for all family members from New York, Paris, and Africa. Dony had succeeded with her logistic abilities to transport and resettle her family of four children from her home in Washington to a beautiful house on Muthaiga Crescent in Nairobi, there to join her husband John, by now Country Director of East Africa for the World Bank.

In December 2009, Lavinia and Michael were busy with their work in New York until Christmas eve. Fiamma's last exam at Barnard College was on the 23rd, as was Tristan's at the Lycée. On the occasion of my 90th birthday on December 8, 2009, Michael sent me to Africa business class.

In her invitation to Africa for Christmas 2009, Dony's motivation was not only pride but also the desire to be with Lavinia, to whom she always appealed in case of need. Dony definitely seemed to have more faith in Lavinia than in me. And it was Lavinia, with her boundless generosity, who helped me during the weeks before my departure in preparing all details of my voyage including a huge suitcase teeming with gifts from the Napanoch *Bambino Gesù* to the "African" family. With her practical spirit and her truly exceptional sensitivity Lavinia felt sure I would face Africa again, as I always had in the past, as a personal adventure, eventually inventing a story about it after my return. The family journey to Africa in 1994 had been the first step the family had taken into a completely new world that Ray and I had never envisaged not even from afar. It had been a breakthrough in a new direction that made me believe that the education of our new family had worked miracles.

While my plane was flying over a dark ocean, I mused about the family we had built, the "education" we had given them that had prepared them to repeatedly break through new frontiers. Could the myth of our Napanoch Christmas be revived again for the family in Africa as it had been on Christmas 1994, when we last had visited Dony in Africa, shortly following the Rwandan genocide?

The individual Africans I had met through Dony and John in my visits to Africa had by 2009 accepted our family's Christmas myth in its entirety and had generously made room for it within their own reality. Peter, the guard, had personally helped me to implement the "Napanoch myth" for my six-year-old grandson Lucas who called himself a Kenyan and spoke a heavily inflected Kenyan English.

When I finally reached Kenya, I encountered a "real" Africa as Dony's gift for my birthday. Her gift centered on a pre-Christmas visit to Il Ngwesi Masai in Northern Kenya, to a magnificent modern lodge, which had housed among its guests the Prince of Wales and his friends. It was dramatically different from the society I had met with Dony the journalist in 1993, 1994, and 1995.

Seen in sequence, and as a whole, my visits to Kenya from 1993 on substantially contribute not only to my 2009 visit but also to my last visit in July 2012 which I spent in the company of eight-year-old Lucas together with the guard Peter, the cook Hellen, the gardener...and the rest of the Kenyans managing Dony's household. I remember one guard in particular who helped Lucas and me compile a list of trees and flowers from the magnificent oasis surrounding the house and who helped us print it out, scientifically identifying each plant and flower with the help of a book from John's library. Most of the trees we discovered had been imported from the Caribbean. I also remember the long hours I spent with Peter the guard, who, together with Lucas, enjoyed every detail of the Arthurian legends I read them and asked me for permission to take the book home to read it to his children. I ended up establishing a direct communication with Peter's village outside Nairobi, and Peter's regular letters witness a friendship between families beyond the ocean that Ray and I had crossed to reach Europe.

Exactly one month after my return from Nairobi in early February 2010, I was taking my usual walk down the hill from the house in Napanoch, along the long winding road that connects us with Yagerville. At twenty-five degrees Fahrenheit, the road was a sheet of ice, the sky a metallic blue, the color of deep winter, the naked arms of the trees stretched stiff against the cobalt backdrop. The whole world, steeped deep in silence, broken only by the cawing of crows, black shadows darting through the blue, usually invited me to relax and enjoy the magic of our winter. Today, the icy wind blowing straight into my face forced me to fumble with my hands, uselessly as usual, to tie the hood of Dony's jacket over my head. Dony had taught me the trick the day she had given me that jacket, but today I was incapable of doing it on my own. As I moved slowly, the wind blew Dony back to me, not the Dony I had just left in Nairobi, but the Donatella she was then, full of carefree, naïve enthusiasm and easy laughter, in one of the happiest coincidences of her life. A child who had discovered the moon.

It had been late fall 1992. In a flurry of colorful details, she reminded me how she bought that expensive Marmot jacket when the New York Times had transferred her from a boring office in Brooklyn to the exciting Police Headquarters. There she had to work with cops in icy winds at every hour of the day and night. While she had enjoyed working with them for a while, the jacket would now be totally useless to her.

"My future is Africa" she announced forcefully. Then she embraced me, took off her Marmot and threw it over my shoulders.

A week later she called us from Africa. She barely had had time to drop off her baggage in a Nairobi hotel, the city where she was supposed to live, that she was dispatched to Somalia to cover a war. For any news or updates, she told us, we should turn to the New York Times. In Napanoch, Lucy led us in prayers for her godchild Donatella. "Africa," she commented, "seems more dangerous than Afghanistan."

"That girl is made for open spaces," Ray had remarked when the family was complaining of the risks Dony was taking even before graduation. "We must let her fly off when she has a chance as long as she can support herself and be properly insured for the risks she takes."

Dony had indeed supported herself in Pakistan on a fellowship while completing a Masters at Columbia in Indic Studies. After graduation, with no financial support from home, a new Dony had suddenly emerged, like Venus from the waves of the sea. The sea in her case was Peshawar, a city at the Khyber Pass that led directly from Pakistan into Afghanistan. From

hundreds of her letters that complemented her articles in the
New York Times, for which she worked as a stringer, she
connected us with her world: an Afghanistan occupied by the
Russians, governed from Kabul by Najibullah, their puppet.
Among the many places she visited beyond the Khyber Pass,
Kabul and the roads that lead to it through the rocky, deserted
Himalayan range seemed to be her favorite targets. She was
always escorted through enemy territory by some Afghan
resistance warriors called *mujaheddins*, or *muj* for short, who
operated under Abdul Haq, one of the five commanders of the
Afghan Resistance who was headquartered in Peshawar. Osama
Bin Laden also makes a cameo appearance in her letters, a kind
of Arab fanatic enjoying unlimited financial support from the
"wrong" Arabs. I remember one of her visits to Kabul, on my
birthday in December, being endlessly protracted because the
muj, who had smuggled her in, were having a hard time getting
her out. She finally made it out, after a week of aborted attempts,
posing as a deaf-mute Afghan bride on her way home after her
wedding in Kabul.

In New York and Napanoch the family followed her step by
step, enthralled by her experiences, reading and rereading her
letters and relating them to her articles. Lavinia was mainly
concerned about getting her insured. As a stringer, we were
informed by the paper, Dony was not covered by the New York
Times, and the cost of insuring a young woman in a war zone—
which only Lloyds of London would consider doing— was the
same as insuring a super tanker, and Lloyds needed two weeks'
notice. The Russians had systematically mined every viable road
between Pakistan and Afghanistan. Abdul Haq himself had lost
a foot that had been replaced by a prosthesis in New York. I
decided I should go to Peshawar to see Dony and check up on
the situation for myself. Ray was by then very ill and my main
academic project at that moment, the complicated deals between
Columbia and the Italian Government for the creation of an
Italian Academy for Advanced Studies at Columbia, had called

for my presence in Rome. Yet, since Ray assured me he was sufficiently cared for by Lavinia and Lucia, in late fall 1988 I left for Peshawar.

Donatella's familiarity with the complicated political situation of Afghanistan and her exceptional personal contacts with the Afghan Resistance made my visit to the area one of the most exciting experiences of my life.[1] By living for two weeks in daily contact with the refugee camps that were home to five million souls, and by often being a guest in refugee tents, with Abdul Haq besides Dony as my guide, I witnessed firsthand the genuine relation of the Afghans to their land and their heroic fight to reconquer it. Abdul Haq was ready to die for the freedom of his country. Several years later, in 2001, when the Americans were heavily involved in Afghanistan, he was killed by the Taliban.

My respect for Dony and for her work during my stay in Peshawar overcame all the doubts I had shared with the family on the legitimacy of her actions. An Afghan taxi driver in New York had once assured me that Dony was very well known among the Afghans in New York. She deserved, I told the family, our (and the New York Times') full support. But Dony had to write something that would justify a possible official recognition of her work by her employer. After ten days in Peshawar and thirty hours of flight on Pakistan Airways, I landed in New York with a rash all over my body and a copy of Dony's article, "Target Kabul", that would appear in December 1988 in the New York Times Magazine. Abdul Haq was the last foreign guest who visited Ray at Riverside Drive in February 1990, shortly before Ray's death. Lucia insisted we should keep him for dinner, whispering to me "*quel povero afgano non si può*

---

[1] See MDP Lorch "A letter from Peshawar" in "Spazio Umano", Milan 1993

mica mandarlo via senza cena!" ("That poor Afghan! We cannot send him away without any dinner!")

"We have to learn to take her as she is. That is how she works at her best..." Ray commented in December 1989 when Dony was already a regular at the New York Times. He played the piano for the last time in honor of his little girl in love with open spaces, on her birthday, February 12, 1990.

The Early Stages

Donatella was ten years old when she broke the ice with me about her intentions to move beyond the usual family turf of Europe. It was one evening in the *Petit Port* of Saint Tropez, where we were staying following the marriage of her sister Claudia, my eldest daughter. She informed me that she intended to explore the world from now on with a backpack and using only public transportation. Later on, as a student of the French Lycée in New York, Vietnam had become her first interest through Michael Herr's *Dispatches* that I had bought for her. Since there were no classes in Vietnamese when she matriculated at Barnard, as a sophomore she settled for Chinese, fighting hard with a non-European language, first at Middlebury College's Summer Session and then, upon graduation, for an entire year in Taipei where she supported herself by teaching English and where she dutifully recorded all her Asian experiences in her daily letters. A year after her graduation, in December 1983, we joined her in Hong Kong where she applied to Columbia's Graduate School within the Department of Indic Studies.

In the early eighties we had been told that as foreigners we would have been allowed to travel through China only in groups with an official guide approved by Beijing. The week after Christmas 1983, Dony led us on an unforgettable journey to the Guilin Province in Southern China, as our official guide. She boasted this voyage would give her a chance to practice her

Mandarin, a language which unfortunately for us all was hardly spoken in the region we visited.

Africa surfaced in her life in late 1992 as a totally unexpected experience. It had appeared in the family's life in the early 1970's in one isolated episode, in a letter Ray had written to Emperor Haile Selassie of Ethiopia in which he was offering our joint services to the University of Asmara. On that occasion, eight-year-old Dony had expressed her desire to join the Bedouins across the Red Sea. Ray's letter, however, had remained unanswered. A war or a famine in Ethiopia or Eritrea must have overshadowed our offer.Our family never made it to Africa until we followed Donatella on her African experience from the invasion of Somalia in 1992-93, where she tragically lost some of her closest friends to the genocide of Rwanda in April-July 1994 and beyond. She lived through these tragedies, reporting on them daily, from the plane crash in Kigali, where she was the very first journalist to appear, until the end of the ensuing genocide. In Rwanda she contracted cerebral malaria which was luckily diagnosed and treated in a hospital in Paris in June of 1994.

In 1996 we agonized with Donatella over an offer to transfer from the New York Times to NBC as their international correspondent based in London. By that time she had radically changed her opinion of the New York Times. The building no longer felt like a prison to her. The Times had become a family she respected even when she dissented. It had taught her a trade. NBC would certainly give her another dimension, but for us at home a new series of anxieties.

In one of her first tasks as a reporter working for NBC, Dony appeared on the screen, donning helmet and bulletproof vest, from the rooftop of a Baghdad hotel. "The war has started," she informed the watching world while bombs were dropping around her. In the quiet Upper West Side of Manhattan, my doorbell rang. An NBC crew was asking for permission to interview me as Dony's mother in front of a television set. They looked around the dining room and the living room. There was no TV among the antique furniture.

"Where is your TV, ma'am?"

"My husband never wanted any TV around," I explained. "When it finally came it was confined to our nanny Lucia's room, near the kitchen." The crew smiled.

"It would do," they concluded.

While they were placing their equipment over and around Lucia, Dony called.

"What about your safety there where you are?" I asked her.

"Don't worry," she replied curtly. "You are a courageous mother who understands and is proud of her daughter in Baghdad: be brief, to the point, smile, and never question my safety."

"I'm horrified," I responded.

"Why?" she asked laughing. "Ridiculous. A war is a war. Didn't you live through one? I love you, mommy. Now, *don't appear afraid*!"

At NBC Dony had the opportunity to wander wherever there was trouble, and trouble was indeed everywhere—from Kosovo and Sarajevo to India and Pakistan. She would have liked to make a documentary on the permanent fighting in Kashmir, on the high mountains between Pakistan and India, but NBC did not seem enthusiastic about it and so she came home on a brief leave accompanied by an Indian poet who longed to see France. At Dony's request, I had read his poetry, had liked it, and had recommended him to the French authorities in Paris for a visa, which he obtained. Michael that summer had rented a *manoir* in the Dordogne, among castles and caves. And the poet boyfriend lived there as our guest. Once back in London, where Dony was based, she promptly and peremptorily dismissed the Indian boyfriend, charging me with consoling him, which I tried to do by visiting the National Gallery with him.

The Donatella of the 1990's was daring, always open to new experiences, ready to fly from the nest as the occasion presented itself, yet stubbornly keeping in contact with the family.

The most meaningful event of the new century, upon her voluntary return to America, happened in her personal life with marriage, motherhood, and the raising of a family of four children, during four years in Washington.

Donatella's Marriage: to Settle Down or to Wander?

I clearly remember Dony's phone call in 2003. She was living at the time in Washington, bored with the environment and with her latest job, busy with a book she had a contract to complete, *The Lost Boys of Africa*. The characters of her story were some African boys whose story she had followed from the Southern Sudan to Michigan.

With that phone call, John flew into our New York family on the wings of a trio of beautiful Latin-Dutch names: *Johannes Cornelis Maria*. Dony had interviewed John, a lawyer at the World Bank, because he had once written an article of interest to her story on the lost boys of the Sudan. He knew well the Africa that Dony remembered with nostalgia.

Shortly thereafter, Dony introduced him to us simply as "John" with a flurry of details: an extraordinary, self-made man who had landed in Canada with his parents at age eight, had found employment on his own as a teenager working on an onion farm so as to pay for a private Port Colborne high-school. Graduating with honors in Philosophy from the University of Toronto, he had won a prestigious fellowship to earn a doctoral degree in Philosophy from Oxford. There he had married Katie, a Canadian Rhodes Scholar. Back in America, he had obtained a Law degree from Harvard and passed the New York State Bar Examination. After a brief stay in Africa, he had worked for a while in New York, with Katie working at the U.N., before moving back to Africa for a second time. The couple by then had two children, Madeline, born in Nairobi, and Nicholas, born in New York. Their third child, Alexander, was to be born in Mali.

"*Simpatico?*" ("nice, easy-going fellow"), we asked Dony over the phone, obviously overwhelmed by the enthusiasm of her description. She hesitated a bit and then: "There is a tragedy in his life," she replied. Lightning had struck John with Katie's sudden death while she was working for UNICEF in Tanzania and he was teaching Philosophy at the University of Nairobi. John appeared as an extraordinary achiever, flying back from the dark heart of Africa to Thunder Bay, Canada, at the other end of the world, to deliver his wife's body to her parents, and then driving back to Port Colborne on Lake Eerie to temporarily park his three orphaned children with his parents, themselves a couple of strong, resourceful Dutch stock, while he organized his new life. Four years after the tragedy, Dony met John. One year later, to the day, they married in a Washington that was overflowing with cherry blossoms. The following year, almost to the day, Lucas Raymond joined the family.

In what is the shortest and most dramatic love story in the family—Lavinia and Michael's being the longest—Dony gives John Ray's wedding ring in the Church of the Holy Sacrament in Chevy Chase, Washington. As in a fable, they move with their three children into the glass-house John designed, one that soon after makes the cover of the "American Architectural Journal."

John was the last man to enter our family of five women— our daughters Claudia, Lavinia, and Donatella, our nanny Lucia, myself, plus on occasion Ray's daughters, Ingrid and Madeleine—, all flitting around a happy Ray while he was alive, stubbornly holding on to his image after he departed. An old-fashioned family that, had we lived in America or England in the past century, might have inspired a novel by an Alcott or a Jane Austen. John had a personality and a background that distinguished him from the other husbands. Claudia's husband, Bernard, who had fallen into our nest from the passing clouds of the 1968 student riots, had vanished suddenly in the '90's, after eighteen years of marriage to Claudia. Michael, on the other hand, the only American-born among the extant in-laws, had, over the years since 1980, conquered his legitimate place as family patriarch, taking upon himself one responsibility after the other, in particular that of Napanoch. Lavinia and Michael married in 1992, two years after Ray's death. Fiamma was born that same summer while Michael and Lavinia still lived with me. Fiamma was two months old when they bought an apartment of their own in a building contiguous to mine.

During the four years that Dony and her new family lived in Washington/Chevy Chase, I was the only member of the New York/Napanoch contingent who had a chance to witness *in loco* the slow development of the composite family into a unity, with the ups and downs I had known through personal experience during my early years of marriage with Ray.

I learned then to love the back of the house that gave the viewer a unique sense of freedom. It allowed me to enjoy Lucas' discovery of the moon and to paint with him the marvels of the fall colors visible through four glass walls. I also admired John's olympic serenity in keeping a vigilant eye on his family as he gave full attention to the World Bank that was defending itself against charges of corruption. John's greatest admirer was Lucas, who used to tell me, when I picked him up at the World Bank Nursery School, that he was proud to go to school in the same building as his father and that he hoped to work with him some day.

As for Dony, I followed her during those Washington years through the daily routine at home, in her metamorphosis from "Wandering Knight" to *mater familias,* coping with the needs of four children under the age of 12. With her final aim being to educate those children to become responsible citizens of tomorrow, Dony began her life as a mother at 42 by taking care of their elementary needs: she burned the warts off their fingers, regulated their sleep habits, and introduced a healthy diet of fruit and vegetables with one regular meal a day consumed together around the table at dinner. She led them in their schoolwork when requested, proud of their success, harsh when she thought they were not realizing their full potential. John, relieved of the most material responsibilities, acted as the needle of the scale, establishing the equilibrium of the family.

A few years after their marriage, I was religiously led during each of my visits for a whole day outing to a fifty-acre plot of land in Virginia which John and Dony had bought as their future Napanoch. While I walked with Lucas through narrow paths of wild forests, John, Dony and the older children worked at opening clearings for a future house that would be built, I discovered later, upon their return from Africa.

Nomina omina. Rappahannock in Virginia recalled Napanoch in the Catskills for its Indian name as well as its connection to the Civil War. There was also a very personal connection. My exploration of its forests and clearings led by an intensely inquisitive, warm-hearted, and very talkative Lucas, the portrait of Lavinia at his age, evoked for me half a century of forest explorations in Napanoch with my own daughters and then with their children. It took me a while to understand why Dony and John had chosen to leave their home for an assignment for the World Bank. Africa was to help them fund the building of a house in Rappahannock.

More probably, as I see things now at a distance, the Africa that had once led them separately to the brim of a precipice was calling them back, together with their newly built family, because of their experience and their personal interest in its recovery. Both realized that a different Africa from the one they had left would meet them now in 2009 as a married couple, a new East Africa that had matured further in its independence through a decade of bloody, ethnic, internecine wars from which it was painfully recovering. It was the challenge of a new Africa that attracted them.

All the children except for Lucas had been reluctant at first to give up the familiar for the unknown. Lucas greeted Africa enthusiastically like every new place to which he would be exposed. By nature, he was a wanderer like his parents, interested in humanity and in life around him. He soon identified his African friends: a Ridgeback named Biko who would grow up under his eyes from puppy to a gigantic-sized pet, a guard named Peter assigned to the family compound, a cook named Hellen who trained him, a very picky eater in Washington, to eat everything she prepared, and a gardener, Patrick, who taught him to identify flowers and plants, allowing him to sink his feet deep into the freshly-plowed, warm earth of the Nairobi plateau before anything was planted in it.

Lucas' older brother, Alex, instead, when he was Lucas' age had discovered Napanoch as the perfect home:

"I'm from Nairobi, caught in between.
A carpet of Jacaranda flowers
Covering the concrete
Of a once mud-and-sisal town…
From the other side of Africa,
mosquito-infested clinic,
Where my mother gave me life, To the
southern half of Kilimanjaro,
Where she slept and never waked.
I'm from my father's steel and glass box
And the house in the Catskills
That always seemed to be full.
I'm from hours in the "studium"
Listening, transfixed,
To the stories Mamina told me.
I'm from 1984
And The Catcher in the Rye.

I'm from my brother's Algebra,
My sister's European History
And a closet full of hand-me-downs…
I am and I am not Dutch, Canadian, American, African
I am and I am not my mother's son
I am the Niger River […]
I am Niagara Falls…I'm Rome full of memories …
I am the Pacific…
I am Mount Kenya."

In December 2009, after embedding with the U.S. Army Special Forces in the Taliban stronghold of Southeastern Afghanistan, Dony was back in Nairobi for three years with no war on which to report. Political and economic troubles, on the other hand, were of direct interest to her Dutch-Canadian husband and to the World Bank that he worthily represented in East Africa. I was most anxious to discover Dony in her totally new African context, in charge of three stepchildren, ages 12 to 17 and of Lucas, the four-year-old child of her marriage to John.

Memories in Flight

I am off to Nairobi. At the Newark airport, a robust, mature Indian lady named Indira Ghandi, settles me into a wheelchair and whisks me through long lines, checkpoints, security checks, and other obstacles, directly to the business class lounge of my special airline, the old *Avion Paris* now baptized by its new owner *British Airways Open Skies. Nomina sunt substantia rerum* ("names are the substance of things"). I settle my thoughts around those I left behind.

As life around me takes shape over another glass of champagne, we reach the Atlantic. Suddenly, the thought of my 90th birthday, to which too much attention has been given lately in New York, wafts into my thoughts. My mind wanders to Villa Moskau in Merano, the night before the family departure for Rome at the dawn of the War, in October 1939, a month after

Hitler's invasion of Poland. My late sister Francesca and I are sitting on the wide wooden balcony dreaming of our past life in Merano, as the family is about to emigrate to Rome under my leadership. Suddenly, worries of what will meet me in Paris push Rome, Nairobi, and the family in Africa into the background.

Will I be able to help Claudia to face Christmas with faith in the future? She was so happy with us in Nairobi in 1994. Claudia by then had just gone through her own family war in Paris, suddenly abandoned by her husband and left with two young children.

We are in Orly. With a sense of guilt, my thoughts fly back to those I have left behind in Napanoch, especially Fiamma and Tristan in their sadness at my having abandoned them for Christmas. With my two suitcases I am wheeled through the empty airport, floating alone between two worlds. Orly is a desert crossed by cleaning ladies of the third and fourth world. With their carts they leave behind them a trail of not unpleasant, sharp smell of disinfectant. In the foggy darkness of a December dawn Paris prepares to live elegantly the shortest day of the year. I easily find a taxi. The silent and reserved driver picks up speed on the deserted highway and I suddenly feel like a Parisian darting home after a brief absence.

Paris was the first city that meant Europe to me when I returned home for the first time from America with Claude and Claudia in 1950, three years after my departure from Italy as a war bride. To be precise, the first city wasn't Paris but Luxembourg in the heart of Europe. The three of us, Claude, Claudia, and myself, had boarded a student plane which, in the summer of 1950, took twenty-four hours with two re-fuelling stops to reach the Old Continent. I had been proud to take Claude and Claudia along on my dime.

My Paris in 1950 with Claudia and Claude still evokes a sequence of unpleasant experiences, the only pleasant one being my mother joining us to take over Claudia so that Claude and I could enjoy the city. Two-year-old Claudia, who then spoke only English, did not get along with my mother at all until my mother cajoled her into following her from the *Hôtel du Quai Voltaire,* where we lived, to the gardens of the Tuileries. There they found a way to survive together for a whole afternoon in spite of the language barrier. I pushed back those memories as too heavy to carry.

Only in 1958, with Ray, did Paris begin to be my first working connection between the two shores. From 1958 on, for many years, Paris remained our *pied-à-terre* in our travels as a family throughout Europe. In 1958, we also acquired in Paris the necessary background for a future understanding of France's political and social development during the Cold War. By May 1989, at the end of Ray's earthly journey, Paris literally became the relief station for him on our way from Warsaw to Budapest back to New York. Our friend, Antoine Gallimard, stepped in to help us when Claudia, worried about her husband, could not take care of us. It was a tragic moment for Claudia's family, the beginning of sad *via crucis* that led her to raise her family on her own as an English teacher. In 1990, Claudia, from Paris, helped me to accept the blow of Ray's death, as our old family had helped her to take the first step out of the labyrinth.

In 1990, when Claudia and her children were evicted from their elegant apartment at Place d'Iéna after the marshalls had confiscated all her furnishings, we discovered the Marais. Claudia's new home was a comfortable apartment in an eighteenth century building that shared one wall with an old church spared by the Revolution. The discovery of a medieval village in the heart of Paris on the very shores of the Seine, close to the bridges that connect the island of Saint Louis to the Isle de la Cité, shed a radically new light on a city which for a long time had remained for our family the gateway to Europe.

From 1958 until the late 1980's when Rome took over as my center of action in Europe, Paris was for both Ray and myself a center for study and research. However, as of 1990, I mainly dedicated myself to helping Claudia and her two children, Celia and Charles.

My favorite walk in moments of depression and despair always led me from Rue des Archives in the Marais through narrow winding roads to a medieval village around the apse of the church of Saint Gervais on the Seine, at the height of the Isle Saint Louis, where I would stop for a while in a little store that exhibited maps of old Paris throughout its history.

My target was always the little park around the apse of Notre Dame, the *Parvis de Notre Dame,* and my walk usually ended in the Cathedral itself whose gothic elegance and divine music whisked me to the world of peace I was longing for. It was in the *Parvis de Notre Dame* that one spring I discovered to my delight the epitaph of the Italian eighteenth century poet Carlo Goldoni, whose comedies I had directed in the early fifties in the Renaissance theater of the Casa Italiana at Columbia. The epigraph informed me that Goldoni was about to receive the title of *poète du Roy* on the verge of the attack on the Bastille which started the Revolution. I was happy to read he escaped the guillotine and the French Revolution altogether. The family in Paris, due to Claudia's divorce, meant mainly trouble, yet I enjoyed it from beginning to end.

"Madame, on y est: 28 Rue Des Archives." ("Madam, we have arrived.") My silent driver had crossed a silent Paris enveloped in a cold winter fog while I was buried as usual in thoughts of the past. I fumbled to punch in the code to enter the building, and Claudia, still in slippers and nightgown, embraced me.

In December 2009, during the four days I spent with Claudia the fog enveloped the city almost constantly, penetrating our very bones. The usual Christmas crowd pushed us aggressively to enter the gigantic Bon Marché and filled the winding narrow roads with shoppers. Claudia and I, as usual, were pressed to achieve some urgent business that she could not perform on her own —in this case furnish the room, recently emptied by her daughter Celia, which had to be rented by January 1, and organize a dinner that would take place on December 13th, the very evening of my forthcoming arrival in Nairobi. The scope of the dinner was to revive around Claudia a group of friends who could help her pick up her life after a two-year hiatus due to a mysterious illness. Claudia was definitely doing better now and was trying her best to courageously face a revival of activities in her life, while I suddenly felt tired and weak.

The last evening of my stay in Paris, on the 12th of December, I was briefly resting from our feverish work at home waiting for Claudia to come back from shopping. Lonely and bored, I decided to venture away from Rue des Archives. On the wide avenue I welcomed the wind. I needed air. Instinctively, as it happened in the past, I took the road of the islands towards Notre Dame.

The cathedral was filled to capacity with people like me from all over the world who needed to free themselves from the fog of everyday life. As I entered, a familiar medieval music drew me up within the forest of gothic columns, under the sky of gothic vaults, until I stood behind the first row of young, soon-to-be priests, in front of the main altar. As I uncomfortably leaned against a column, one of them, a young adolescent blond, thin as a wafer, gave me his seat and a leaflet which allowed me to follow the ceremony I was witnessing: the medieval Christmas rite of consecration into the priesthood, celebrating not the abnegation but the glorification of the self at the service of others. In my present mood, I felt the rite conducive to a form of freedom that is gained by discovering where one stands in a world that is changing so rapidly one can hardly recognize it as one's own after a night of sleep.

The medieval music penetrated and transformed the Latin text that I followed religiously. The text came alive through the music and the boys who were singing it in that immense gothic cathedral that had been spared by the French Revolution. This otherwise indefinable experience led me to float as in a dream back into the cathedral of my hometown in the Italian Tirol before it was occupied by Hitler's troops. Singing in German their final good-bye to their ancestral land, the farmers were getting ready to leave for cold Bavaria, courtesy of Hitler's agreement with Mussolini. My best friend from school, Hans Haller, along with his five brothers, was killed in the German Army at the siege of Stalingrad. He had written to me in Rome up to the last moment. In the cathedral my mind was abruptly overshadowed by the fleeting image of my sister Francesca and myself, standing on the wooden balcony of our room at the Russian Villa Moskau in Merano, where Mamma and my family had found refuge from the War. On that moonlit night of a golden October, we had said our good-byes to the only land we had known so far. As happened in ancient times before a barbarian invasion, the family had sold all of its earthly possessions and was about to abandon its nest in the Alps for a "safer" Rome. In 1940, Rome was still considered—hard to believe—a bastion of security. I was leading the family to Rome with the support and mentorship of my Latin Professor, the well-known classicist and member of the Italian Academy, Vincenzo Ussani.

As I was lost in old memories, the young men were lining up for communion. I did not join them. My wristwatch called me back to the reality of Claudia waiting for me. I returned the document to the blond young man and rushed back to the exit of the cathedral, cutting my way through the thick and silent crowd that was slowly gliding to the altar to receive communion. Why was I leaving now?, they seemed to reproach me. Didn't I perceive the deep meaning of the rite which called for this final personal participation in it? My destiny called me elsewhere.

Where precisely, I didn't know. I was following my instincts rather than my duty.

On the wide and empty Place de Notre Dame, facing the sculpted façade, a gigantic *Tannenbaum* lifted itself high and strong, frightfully alone, beaten by the wind. A Christmas tree without any ornament and without any manger to protect, enveloped by an impenetrable blue net, blue like the sky behind the fog, like the background of the manger in Napanoch that we painted for our nativity scene. I imagined that gigantic tree carried by the wind from somewhere in the countryside into the heart of a village on the Seine, flown straight from the forests that once encircled the island before Caesar conquered the river for Rome. I stopped in awe. *"Gallia est omnis divisa in partes tres..."* ("All of Gaul is divided into three parts")[2] and *"Pater noster qui es in caelis..."* ("Our father who art in heaven").

At age ten when I memorized those two texts in Latin I certainly did not intuit the deep-rooted and dramatic contrast between the pagan and the Christian worlds. It was the miracle of Dante's poetry, as I discovered it as a young teacher in America, that suddenly led me to recognize the connection between Rome and Christ. That discovery inspired my colleague, Susan Wemple, a medieval historian, and myself, in the 1970's, to create a "Program in Medieval and Early Renaissance Studies" at Barnard College with the support of the National Endowment for the Humanities. The program was based on an interdisciplinary course we had created on the *Divine Comedy* and on a course on Early Renaissance Humanism. It was a poet at the sunset of the Middle Ages who concretely imagined how the two worlds, that of Caesar and that of Jesus, interacted and fused.

Suddenly, a blow of icy wind, harsh, violent, and merciless lifted me away from the Cathedral Square across the Seine, past

---

[2] The opening of the *De Bello Gallico (Gallic Wars)*, Caesar

the *Hôtel de Ville* and the *Bon Marché*, to the safe refuge of 28 Rue des Archives.

"Where have you been for so long? Our Christmas dinner is ready." Claudia, my grandson Charles, and I toasted to future Christmases that might reunite us all in peace and togetherness, as the one we enjoyed in Napanoch or perhaps, Charles ventured, as the unforgettable experience of a Christmas tree in the African N'gwezi Masai Mara.

At six a.m., after a sleepless night, an exceptionally elegant and talkative Parisian taxi driver led me back through the silent dark *ruelles* of a cold, foggy Marais to an empty Orly where only a multilingual and multiracial cleaning crew quietly shuffled around. He stayed with me until a young man opened a counter proudly displaying the sign of *Kenyan Airways*. Like Indira Gandhi at the Newark Airport, my gentleman Parisian driver refused to "abandon" me until the counter gave signs of life. An elderly British gentleman with what I judged to be his tall and elegant black wife seemed to be my only companions in the business class lounge for the flight that connected the heart of Europe to the heart of Africa. By the time I reached the plane, I had acquired five more voyage companions who would sleep throughout the flight.

I had chosen to travel by day because twice in the past I had been royally treated with the view of sea and land—the snowy Alps followed by the familiar Mediterranean, the sea between the lands, with two of its four peninsulas and the islands that surround them. I paid homage to Homer before we reached the moonlit mouth of the Nile, which we followed into the dark mysterious Africa of the Queen of Sheba. This time, however, I had no luck. The congenial hostess who became my guide and companion during the flight—an anticipation of the Kenyans I was about to meet after so many years of absence from Africa—woke me up gently with a late breakfast, whispering to me "Look at the tips of your snowy Alps piercing through the clouds."

After that, a thick grey carpet hid the rest of the Mediterranean until a golden sunset revealed the mouth of the Nile which it followed up to its sources. As night swallowed Africa, I closed my eyes to see once more the first image of Dony at the airport of Nairobi, once upon a time, the first time I had visited her in 1993: a mercurial, shorthaired Dony who found a way of entering the plane shortly after it had landed and of whisking me off. As her car had darted on a straight long road under the equatorial stars to Muthaiga Crescent, she had told me of the many adventures we would live together with her family in Africa.

"Your address in Nairobi, Madame!" The first person I met on African soil on December 18, 2009, was a young man with a business smile in charge of the wheelchair Lavinia had providentially ordered for me. As I told him I had no specific address except an official one, the "World Bank," he changed attitude and with sudden respect he mumbled: "Then some important person will come to fetch you!" As he spoke that important person showed up. I leapt up from the wheelchair and ran, much to the surprise of the young man, to embrace a joyous John who handed me his cell phone to speak with Dony and Lucas.

John's importance did not shorten my exit to freedom because my two red suitcases had to be identified among the hundreds of other red bags that passed by us on the moving belt with hands of all colors stretched out to choose their own. Red seemed to be a popular color in Africa.

The familiar fragrance of jasmine that had been with me since I had first visited Africa hit me as I walked after dinner, alone with Dony, through the vast lawn crisscrossed by flowerbeds, to what was to become my home. Now, for Christmas, in 2009, all the past was absorbed into an intense present as Dony and I walked under the stars, sharing that moment in spirit with Fiamma, Tristan, Michael and Lavinia at "home" in Napanoch.

Beautiful Africa

Among my seven visits to Dony in Africa, from the fall of 1993 to the two-month visit in November/December 2012, I see the first four at the end of the past century like a dream which foreshadows the other three in the new millennium. They are by now visions of a land imbued with memories that make it my own, dear to me because of the land itself and mostly the people I met there. Details surface within a general vision allowing me here and there to give them a mythical meaning. Often more visions than plain visits.

Between 1993 and 2012, I witness in my own family a period of internal transformation following Ray's death, Lavinia's and Michael's marriage in New York, the abandonment of family by Claudia's husband in Paris, the end of my directorship of the Academy.

From the fall of 1993 to the fall of 2012 my own Africa fans out at first in line with the "foreign correspondents" around my youngest daughter Donatella who report on it with courage and purpose, but at a certain distance from the subject.

In my final visit in 2012 I meet the Africans personally in the household of Donatella, mother of a family of four, who reports through USAID on the progress of the Africans, and of my son-in-law John Zutt, the country director of the World Bank for the region.

***

In my world with Ray Africa did not exist. Our world had been strictly limited to a Europe divided in two by Yalta in 1945. Ray died in March 1990 as I was nominated Director of the recently founded "Italian Academy for Advanced Studies," and shortly before the New York Times needed a correspondent for East Africa.

Thus, it happened that after a glorious visit to the Alps of my childhood which I took with Dony as a treat, Dony found herself packing to leave for Nairobi. As I stated with pride in one of the letters I wrote to Ray in his after life, Dony and I were both to begin a new job: she as East Africa Bureau Chief and I as Director of a newly-minted Italian Academy for Advanced Studies in America.

Once in Africa, Dony left immediately for Somalia. As for me, for the first four years I built the Italian Academy within a renovated seven-story building called *Casa Italiana* that was to be inaugurated in 1996. In the meanwhile, beginning in 1992, I would be housed in Columbia's Rare Books and Manuscript Library in Butler Library.

Today my visits to Africa surface in unison, visions from the past millennium, ready for me to revive freely as in the old silk fan my mother treasured which revealed different images according to how you opened it.

From these visions, as I dive deeper into an Africa that stumbles and falls in order to get up again, the visits materialize as I evoke them in chronological sequence through the creative lens of my memory and the more grounded accounts of my diaries.

It was 1993 at the tiny airport of Nairobi, a small town bustling with lively people, tall and slim, and at Dony's home built by a German couple in a kind of forest that surrounds the neighborhood called Muthaiga Crescent. A flock of birdwatchers flies with Dony, her photographer, and myself on a tiny plane over the canyons of Northern Ethiopia. They diagnose the stomach illness of my two companions following a rich dinner in the luxurious home of the most prominent lady in Addis Ababa. Here is the doorman of the *Hôtel Milles Collines* in Kigali embracing Dony and me. His whole family had been killed by the Hutus.

As Dony and I walk to our room overlooking the City of Hills, I hear the voice of Keith Richburg from an article Dony read to me again and again from The Washington Post of March 1995: "I watched the dead float down a river in Tanzania. Of all the gut-wrenching emotions I wrestled with covering famine, war, and misery in America no feeling so gripped me than the scorching hot day last April, standing on the Rosumu Falls Bridge in a remote corner of Tanzania, watching dozens of discolored bloated bodies floating down stream, floating from the insanity that was Rwanda. I know exactly the feeling that haunts me [...] somewhere, sometime, maybe four hundred years ago an ancestor of mine was shackled in leg irons and put with thousands of other Africans into the crowded filthy cargo hold of a ship for the long treacherous journey across the Atlantic [...] I thank God my ancestors made that voyage. I have covered the famine and civil war in Somalia. I've seen a cholera epidemic in Zaire [...] I have interviewed evil 'warlords,' I have encountered machete-wielding Hutu mass murderers [...]. Now after three years I am beaten down and tired."

I went back to my room at the Hilton, turned on CNN and learned that my Italian journalist friend Ilaria Alpi and her young cameraman, had been killed in a shoot-out in Mogadishu." As Dony reads, I hear the horror and challenges of her experiences and of those of all reporters.

Here is the slim body of Dan Eldon, Dony's young photographer friend, being dragged behind a truck in Somalia. Dony calls me to tell me, as I am on a deserted beach in Crete, immersed in Homer's Iliad. I seek out a phone to call Dan's mother Kathy in California. Dan Eldon was the youngest of the four journalists killed. Luck, circumstances, or simply the fact that Dony had stayed home that evening from exhaustion, had saved her from the massacre.

Dawn found me walking along Homer's sea in an attempt to reconcile myself with humanity. The first line of the *Iliad* that I had been reading to my grandchildren, Celia and Charles, on the beaches of Crete came to me with the music of the waves, *Menin aeide Thea…* ("O Goddess sing the wrath of Achilles, son of Peleus"). Wrath (*menin,* in Greek) was the cause of the tragedy. Achilles asked his mother for revenge. Thetis, a goddess, knew that by giving into his request and providing her son with new arms she would bring the day of his untimely death closer. Yet, faced with her son's pain and humiliation that had been provoked by Agamennon, general of the Greek army, she does not have the courage to break the iron circle of rage and of war. She yields. Her act embitters the war. Achilles will kill Hector, the just defender of the Trojans, all the while aware that he himself will be killed shortly thereafter. Homer was indeed the first war correspondent.

My mind flies back to Nairobi, to the interview of the Italian journalist Benni who seemed to have an answer as to why we bombed the starving Somalis instead of feeding them as we had promised. My mind is swarming with the presence of Africa. Here is the whole Napanoch family cutting a "Christmas Tree" in the heart of Africa, discovering step by step a new born Kenya in three interconnected safaris in the "Heart of Darkness." Here is Kigali a year after the genocide, celebrating peace and life through journalists in picturesque confusion, and here Ethiopia spreads from the marvels of Addis Abeba to the grottoes of Lalibela, the obelisks and the stele of Axum, and Nairobi again…. Nairobi as the center of our life in a final goodbye party to those *wandering knights* of today who have become by 1995 my dearest friends. What I see is an Africa that courageously fights to deserve its independence.

Dony and I traveled together, riding at night from one colleague's residence to another, all buried in the thick green vegetation of the Kenyan plateau. Wherever Dony took me, I found myself at the center of a group of "young wandering knights" who were always on the go, their horse ready to take them from clearing to clearing in the "thick forests" of East

Africa. *Wandering Knights* is what these foreign correspondents were and they in turn declared me to be not their *Angelica*, the princess pursued by the knight Orlando in the *Orlando Furioso*, which was supposedly East Africa, but their adopted mother, and they treated me as such.

During my next visit in January 1994, with Dony and her closest friend Josh Hammer, we took off on an unforgettable "adventure" to Zambia, Lake Victoria, and Victoria Falls. In Lusaka, capital of Zambia, Dony and Josh interviewed Kenneth Kaunda, independent Zambia's first President. Following the interview, the stately old gentleman asked to chat with me about his wife's illness. He spoke of the solitary life he lived, cut off from his people whom he missed and, with a spark in his eyes, he spoke of his personal friendship in better days with the Italian Prime Minister Giulio Andreotti. I told him of my own friendship with Andreotti before the project Academy had surfaced, as we worked together in the warm creative atmosphere allowed by the Center for International Scholarly Exchange (CISE) that I had founded, an independent organization of faculty from Barnard and Columbia, a center that bloomed as a family of scholars working together in shared courses across the Atlantic. Long before I envisioned the project Italian Academy, in fact, Andreotti and the Italian President, Cossiga, had joined CISE as scholar partners and had participated in conferences focusing on the Italian Constitution.

After Dony and Josh finished interviewing the soccer coach, sole survivor of a soccer team that perished in a plane accident, we sailed together along the widest and richest river I had ever laid eyes on, the Zambesi, that flowed into Victoria Falls. Crocodiles surfaced by our boat as we sipped a pink cocktail. That was my baptism into the complexities of Africa as well as into the life of foreign correspondents in action, friends and competitors at the same time.

The Christmas 1994 family visit alongside my visit of 1995 are emblazoned in my memory as two sides of the same coin. It was the massacre of five reporters on July 13, 1993, in the heart of Mogadishu that inspired the Italian Academy's Workshop "Somalia, Rwanda and Beyond: The Role of the Media in an International Perspective." Our workshop on February 14, 1994, with the contribution of Louis Boccardi of the Associated Press, the CBS anchor Dan Rather and Sir Brian Urquhart, among others, was the product of my ensuing friendship with Dan Eldon's mother Kathy who was the living spirit behind the event.

The workshop and exhibit were originally dedicated to Dan and the other three journalists who had been killed. Yet, by virtue of the cause they were upholding, which was peace, we at the Academy had decided to dedicate the event not only to them but to all those who died in Somalia in the famine that preceded international intervention and to all those who subsequently died on both sides of the fence that suddenly rose between some Somalis and the UN soldiers and relief workers.

The book that followed in 1995, "*Somalia, Rwanda and Beyond: The Role of the International Media in Wars and Humanitarian Crises*" was a means for the Italian Academy and all that it stood for to officially recognize the women and men who humbly and courageously connect us at home with those places in the world where tragedy overwhelms the innocent. It was the reportage from these journalists that stirred us to face the complexity of the issue.

Dony on duty was more exciting than Dony on vacation. She is by nature at her best in action. And so am I, I discovered in those years as we worked together side by side. In December 1995 I completed my visits to Africa under Donatella's leadership with a Thanksgiving in a finally peaceful Kigali, at the *Hôtel Mille Collines* which at the onset of the killing had relieved me of the anguish of not knowing Dony's whereabouts in that bloody event.

November 2, 2010

Dear Ray,

Today our spring is dry, as it often happens after a dry summer. Today is the day of the dead. My first memory of a cemetery, a place my mother hated and never visited, is in my home in the Alps. A tiny, fragile, ten-year-old, freezing under the rain, in fascist uniform amid many other girls like her. That little girl is me. Everyone is listening to a military band that evokes the noise of the guns in the trenches of a long war to whose end they owe their life: *"tapum tapum tapum."* That was World War I.

Today, after work, I went to church to pray. I have left an army of dead behind me. Not you. You are for me today, as always, beyond me and behind me. To revive my spring I have to dig, as we did together in the past in Napanoch during the droughts, dig into our personal story, searching for the origin of that *beyond*.

Today, I saw the two of us back in October 1983 on a beach in Rio de Janeiro. Nelida Piñon and a Brazilian writer friend of hers have invited us to celebrate with them the end of my series of lectures on Dante in Brazil. That very day I had closed my final lecture at the Federal University with the aged Ulysses of Canto XXVI. Fired by *"l'ardor di divenir del mondo esperto/ e de li vizi umani e del valore"* ("the burning desire to become experts of the world, of human vice and valor"), Ulysses boldly inspires his "old and tired" companions who had left Ithaca, to cross beyond Gibraltar, to undertake the ultimate adventure of their lives. After five months of exciting navigation, just as land, a high mountain, appears on the horizon, a whirlwind hits the little skiff, turning it three times upon itself, until the Ocean swallows it: "*Infin che il mar fu sopra noi richiuso*" ("until the sea was closed upon us").

That memorable October night, in front of our little restaurant of Copacabana, the Atlantic roared under a full moon, a mysterious expanse of water. You Ray, the scientist, provided us humanists with the description of that mysterious infinity in the words of the Arab Al-Idrisi. Born near Gibraltar at the dawn of the past millennium, he was a famous cartographer and geographer whose maps were consulted by Vasco De Gama and Christopher Columbus. He had written that "No one knows what is in that sea because of many obstacles to navigation, profound darkness, high waves, frequent storms, innumerable monsters which people it and violent winds. They limit themselves to sail along the coast without losing sight of the land."

Do you remember, Ray? The tasty fish and spicy wine that inspired us all with Ulyssean ardor. The angry, tempestuous Ocean under a full moon filled us with respect and fear for Al-Idrisi's holy monster. Nelida's recounting of an Africa and South America joined and then split apart by a pre-historic tectonic movement led us into a world where reality interwove seamlessly with fantasy. I don't remember how, when and which one of our two Brazilian friends suddenly turned to me with a proposal that sounded like an order: "You should plan a novel based on the fascinating story of your Ulysses. A story inspired by the Ocean that roars at our feet, ready to swallow us while we burn with the desire of taming it, a novel on … Beyond Gibraltar."

"Why Beyond Gibraltar?" I asked. "Because that's where you led us with your lecture."

You and I briefly spoke about the idea of a novel on the plane back to New York. You suggested that I concretize, through the story of my original family across the Ocean, that *beyond* as the challenge of living life as intensely as possible. You were gripped by the adventures of my widowed mother who raised her four children in a small town in the Tyrol, by the family's survival of the War in Rome, and by my final leap beyond Gibraltar. Your death made that *beyond* real to me the way my father's death had made his to my mother. Our own life together from the moment we met on a golden October day in 1951 to the moment you left me in March 1990—entering, in your own words, "a sweet sunset"—developed in my imagination into a series of unexpected sequences of *beyonds*.

I have found the water of our spring. Thank you for being the only person in the world who listens to me when I desperately need to express myself. Love as always.

***

October 12, 2010

Dear Fiamma,

Barnard Alumnae Magazine a few months ago published an article about our family as a "Barnard Family" and featured a photo of four of us: you, your mother, your aunt Madeleine, and myself on the cover. (Dony and Claudia's pictures appear in the background, as does that of your great aunt, Ray's sister, Tante Madeleine).

What did Barnard teach us as a "Barnard Family?" What it taught me as a woman besides as a teacher, during my half-century of service, is something not even a war had taught me before I landed in New York in 1947. Barnard made me aware of the meaning and importance of existing. To *exist* means to realize the best of oneself without fear or limits, while respecting not only the law of the land and the judgment of peers, but the universal moral law that calls for the fulfillment of our obligations towards other human beings. Nobody but the family that gave us birth can teach us how to love the little boy who dies of neglect in Africa or in the Bronx. Love of our neighbor starts at home. Your mother is a product of that lesson.

The article does not say that you, who literally owe your life to Barnard, where your grandparents fought and won the battle to build a new family together, are carving for yourself a unique path which is very different from the one that inspired your grandparents, mother, and aunts. What makes me proud of you is the thought of your having chosen as fulfillment of your science requirement an extraordinary course that calls for your whole self, day and night: a study of the Hudson from the glacial era to today, carried out through "Environmental Studies" which cover the sciences, history, and literature. This is indeed a path that none of us had contemplated. I fell in love with the Hudson shortly after my arrival on its shores, in 1947, and then decided to pitch my tent on its shores. Only Barnard, through your Professor Bower, could have given you this extraordinary possibility.

Exactly five hundred years before your birth, on the very day of your birth, Christopher Columbus was gathering his caravels in Gomera, what he considered the best port in the Canary Islands, for his departure for the unknown across the Atlantic. Why Gomera? Why the Canaries? Gomera, Columbus knew, offered abundant water, meat, and wood that, as admiral, he judged indispensable to the great crossing of the Atlantic. By studying Columbus' life closely, I discovered that he prepared his grandiose project with unparalleled accuracy, not in order to satisfy his sponsors, Queen Isabel and King Ferdinand, but because it was in his own very nature to plan so precisely.

Many navigators before Columbus had tried the Crossing and some had shipwrecked like Dante's Ulysses. Columbus is the very first explorer who not only succeeded but did so safely and thus opened a secure road for millions of future emigrants.

Before seeking the sponsors for his project Columbus for years had made the Ocean the personal laboratory for his studies, from Iceland to the African coast, and he had, of course, spent a long time in the Canary Islands. Columbus had had no schooling whatsoever. He spoke the Genovese dialect of his parents and had learned on his own to speak and write Castilian and Portuguese. What he also learned on his own, by experience, was the art of navigation. What helped him the most is to have set up with his brother Bartolomeo a cartography shop in Genova which forced him to explore in order to create the maps. This is what Paolo Emilio Taviani, an Italian Minister at the time of the kidnapping and assassination of the Prime Minister, Aldo Moro, told me.

Nobody taught you, Fiamma, how to organize your studies as you do, not even your mother who has been and remains your ideal teacher in many ways. You make your choices as if inspired by a dream. You have taught yourself to move slowly and securely, step by step, towards whatever goal you have set. Perhaps you do not have as of yet a final goal, as most people of your age do not....

Taviani admired his co-citizen for having prepared, step by step, the long road towards his successful landing on the island he called San Salvador on October 12, 1492. While I celebrated Columbus' quincentennial, as the first Director of the newly founded Italian Academy, Taviani kept on warning me "Do not invent. Exploit reality." My reality at the time was a little girl called Fiamma Lucia, born precisely on Columbus' quincentennial. So I mentioned you more than once. Love, your Mamina.

New York, September 8, 2010

Dear Lucas,

Since your departure I try in vain at night to find some stars we might share. Somehow our stars here seem to be different from yours. Perhaps we could tell each other stories about stars. I remember your mommy, Donatella, at your age. She was a quiet girl, in appearance at least. Well tucked into bed at night near Lavinia, she would ask me to tell her a story, and then another story, and then one more. I told her stories of old times about fantastic people on fantastic islands, on new lands. My students to whom I told those stories during the day seemed to like them as much as your mommy did at night. The story I'm sending you today is not of that kind, although it takes place on one of those star-planets that paint a shining carpet every night above our head. Your mother would have liked it when she was your age.

With all my love, Mamina

The fable of three magic bracelets

The old woman of our story flew from planet Earth to another planet. There she married a man who adored her. Their planet, called Venus, was as beautiful as a planet can be, rich in flowers and butterflies, birds and all sorts of animals, precious stones and gold.

Together with her husband whom she loved dearly the woman raised three daughters, one more beautiful than the other. In harmony with their planet, the parents had called them Stella, Sole, and Luna. The language they spoke at home was neither English nor French nor Italian; not even Arabic or Swahili. It was an old language forgotten on the planet Earth.

Venus was also rich in books in all languages the girls could understand because they knew Latin and Greek which are secret keys that open many worlds.

As for gold, there was so much of it around Venus that people did not bother about it except for a rare quality, well known because it magically connected a mother with her children throughout their entire lives no matter how far apart they ever lived.

The woman of this story and her husband lived happily with their daughters for many years without giving them any jewels at all. Instead, they gave them green meadows and a forest full of animals where they could play to their heart's content, and many books to read. One day the old husband close to death secretly called the middle daughter Sole, and asked her to visit an old jeweler friend of his who, he knew, still had a bit of that precious magic gold.

"After my death," he told her, "your mother will need to feel her daughters close to her no matter where they live. Go and see Vulcan, my old friend the jeweler, and ask him kindly on my behalf to shape, out of the magic gold I know he still owns, three bracelets that your mother will wear as long as she lives. Each one the same in shape but of a different color of gold—white, yellow, and red."

Sole, who had decided as a young girl she would never leave Venus for good, ran to Vulcan who, as a jeweler, was also known as Mr. Goldminer. He was a great admirer of how the two parents had raised their daughters keeping them close to them, even when their destiny called them to build a family far from home. By then, Stella the eldest, had already flown back to their parents' original planet Earth to raise her family there. Luna, the youngest, had given clear indication that she would fly as far as she could through the wide blue sky. Luna was the daughter about whom the wise father worried the most.

Mr. Goldminer received Sole warmly. Shortly thereafter he delivered to her three magic bracelets, each made of a slightly different colored gold. In a touching ceremony on his wife's birthday the old father gave the three bracelets to his wife. The three daughters swore they would keep close to their mother and visit her at least once a year all together on the home planet, no matter where their destiny took them. The mother for her part swore that from that moment on she would keep those bracelets on her left arm making sure that they were always safely in place. Every time she touched them it felt as if she were embracing all three of her daughters.

The three bracelets were of a rare beauty, thin and so exceptionally elegant in shape and color that everybody admired them.

Years passed with no change in the family relationship. On a beautiful summer day, the old mother and her eldest daughter were traveling by car from a visit to the village near their summer home, when the old woman noticed that one of the magic bracelets was missing. Greatly upset, she begged Stella to turn back immediately to the village. She refused to go home without the bracelet. Stella, however, kept on driving as if nothing had happened.

"You haven't lost the bracelet at all," she smiled peevishly.
"Look under your seat. I see it there."
"How can you see it while driving?" the mother asked.
"It is reflected in the stars!" Stella laughed. She stopped the car and picked up the bracelet from under her mother's seat.

The two embraced. The mother tucked the precious bracelet in the inner pocket of her purse. She did not trust her luck until consulting her old friend the jeweler.

"All this bracelet needs," the old jeweler told the anxious mother when, one month later, she brought it to him to have it fixed, "is an extra security pin, but can you please tell me what happened between you and your daughters shortly before the bracelet escaped you?"

The old woman thought hard before answering.

As an astrologist and a psychologist besides a jeweler, Mr. Goldminer pressed the old lady until she admitted that something had indeed happened between her and her daughters, but she did not specify when.

"From now on, if you want the magic of the bracelets to work," the old man stated solemnly, shaking his crest of white hair, "when they all come home to visit, give these daughters of yours the necessary space to feel truly free even if that means..."

"I understand..." the woman interrupted.

"Magic," he continued as if to himself, looking out of his shop at the orange-purple sky at sunset, "can help, but it needs human support."

The three magic bracelets dangling at the mother's wrist were whispering to each other in harmony as the old jeweler, tall and hunched over, and the tiny woman, straight as an arrow, walked home together happily under the stars.

New York, Palm Sunday 2011

My dear Ray,

Today, our fifty-fifth wedding anniversary, I relive in my memory with fondness and some apprehension the day of our wedding. It was Palm Sunday 1956, in Tenafly, at the home of your parents. Witnesses to our marriage were your mathematician friend Howard Levy and my sister Bona. Both had faith in our marriage as a new beginning. In the background, equally supportive, were those colleagues who had stood by us in the trying years of separation and divorce, Thomas Peardon,

Dean of the Faculty of Barnard College, and Millicent McIntosh, Dean of the College.

When I met you, you were teaching a course on "Functional Analysis" and one on "Quantum Theory." I was teaching "Dante" in Elementary and Intermediate Italian. That was back in the middle of the past millennium. Today I wonder how successful we have been in building our family.

Our three daughters, who lived with us and on whom we focused most of our attention during the first twenty years of our married life, now live in three different continents, Europe, Africa, and America. The dialogues among the three remain intense and lively.

We met our faithful nanny Lucia in Rome on Easter, 1958, as we left Paris for Rome to visit my mother. It was an epic ride that lasted two weeks, in our overloaded little Austin, on old roads of Roman origin still bearing the wounds of four years of recent bombardments. Lucia was a middle-aged woman of great beauty, charm, and unbelievable dedication to the family. She was living at the time in a boarding house in Rome. She could speak French as well as Italian, having spent thirty years as governess in the beautiful *Villa Mon Désir* in Nice raising the daughter of the French King of Sugar, "*Le Roi du Sucre*," Jacques Lebaudy. When Lebaudy, after a long period of insanity in New York, was killed in their Long Island home by his wife Augustine, known as M'amie, for having molested their daughter Jacqueline, M'amie made her way back to France, but not before spending some time in a New York jail and becoming addicted to morphine. As general household manager of the Lebaudy estate, Lucia would accompany M'amie during the years preceding the War and throughout the War itself, to the Casino of Monte Carlo, and she would recount with relish her adventures there with Guido, the chauffeur, who was sent on missions to replenish the supply of morphine. Lucia would tell of the sleepless nights she spent with M'amie who chain smoked in her room on Nice's *Corniche Fleurie,* and of adopting with M'amie, from the neighboring hamlet of La Palud, another young girl, Dany, who had been orphaned of her mother and left in the care of her alcoholic father.

These Gatsby-esque experiences clashed with Lucia's own upbringing. Having lost her father in a motorcar accident at age three and her mother at age eight from Spanish influenza, she had been sent early on to a religious boarding school by her stepfather who himself died when Lucia was twelve. Although she spent summers with dozens of similarly orphaned cousins in her grandmother's rambling manor surrounded by rice paddies near Verona, it had become clear to her early on that she should enter the novitiate. Just as she was about to take her final vows, however, Lucia realized that she was made more for a life of action than one of contemplation. And so it was that she found her way to Nice in the late 1920's. Yet no matter how many years she spent accompanying M'amie to gamble in casinos and arrange for morphine deliveries, Lucia never lost a deep and grounded sense of faith.

When we met her in Rome, Lucia had just discovered that the man she was about to marry was actually homosexual. Distraught, she was living in a religious *pensione* (boarding house), attending mass at six every morning.

Lavinia fell in love with Lucia at first sight and Lucia, who was made for children, found her *raison d'être.* Donatella literally owes her life in 1962 to Lucia's presence in our family. She became Donatella's godmother and supported her adventures, sometimes even without our knowing it.... Keeping Lucia legally in the United States, however, called for true ingenuity on our part and a thorough understanding of the ever-changing immigration laws. From a tourist visa, she obtained a student visa, studying make-up arts under the Russian actress, Tamara Daykarhanova, a consultant for the Barnard theatre. Finally, in 1965, we celebrated her green card. Never truly learning English, she was bound to live with us, overseeing our picturesque household for the rest of her life from March 26, 1958, to March 26, 2001. She died in her bed, surrounded by pictures of all the children and all their own children which she had helped raise.

***

Napanoch, Memorial Day Weekend, 2011

My dear Ray,

I am writing to you from Napanoch on Memorial Day Weekend. Summer is suddenly here. Or the end of Spring moving into Summer, a Spring in full bloom… from the daffodils rapidly replaced by the lilacs to the wild azaleas and the magnolias (Michael's recent contribution) soon to be replaced by the mountain laurel which, as you remember, will envelop the whole forest around the houses with its delicate white and pink bridal veil.

John and Junior, our faithful caretakers, the van Burens, father and son, Mr. Brooks, his wife and children, plus some specialists of flowers and animals come and go on the lawn around the houses to confabulate with Michael and Lavinia, while Fiamma and Tristan are somewhere down in the meadow around the pond, or more probably helping John with the animals or busy working the vegetable garden, fenced in like a camp of pioneers, with one of the many machines with which Michael has enriched the property. Each one has a special name. There are huge machines that dig, mow grass, or cut trees. The thirty storm windows of the house are down in a jiffy, replaced by the summer screens, Vinnie's work as usual. Precisely like in the old days, from 1964 on.

The Family Book on Memorial Day in the seventies reads: "Today *fervet opus*" (work is buzzing). Written by Lavinia…. Work today is as fervent as in the past but is performed more efficiently, to say the least, and with much more noise. I help here and there in easy chores like raking or gardening.

I wander into the forests that blanket the mountain with a thick net of fresh green. I walk and walk.... "Aren't you afraid of getting lost?" you used to ask me. But you know my answer. Like in the old days, I laugh.

Nobody around here has time to listen to the birds, so many of them hidden in the tender new foliage, to the woodpecker and so many others I distinguish by sight and sound. I do not know their names in any language. I wish Fiamma, who is majoring in "Environmental Studies" and just took a marvelous course on "birds", would come with me, but I haven't dared ask her. When she does not study she is working, a fabulous organizer of the household and the property. I remember Claudia's son Charles as a little boy and even his semi-wild sister Celia exploring with me in the past century the area we called *I Prati* (The Meadows), covered with berries of all kinds. But now Charles is a banker working close to the President of La Banque De Paris et Pays Bas in Paris and Celia works in a European firm.

I guess birds are for them a memory from the Past. Fourteen-year-old Tristan, tall, straight, and frail like the most elegant of our birches, is my only companion, but he is approaching his "Bac" which means studying literature, history, and the social sciences of France as a member of the European Community— and of course America as well—, plus math and the natural sciences. No time for walks.

Of course, he shares his studies with his mother, as Fiamma did over the years—an essential aspect of family life today. As for Lucas, I didn't spend enough time with him in Napanoch to get him to love the forests and to explore them with me. It will be for a next time. I hope not too late.

Musings on the Winter Solstice

New York, Saturday, December 20, 2010

I still do not understand the contours, the individual stories, that may illustrate this new myth, but I sense that I am in a state of grace which can be identified as a state of "folly," awakened in me by the warmth of the environment.

In 1963, I seek out "a House in the Wilderness" without a clear understanding of what we really needed in order to create a new family. We proceed unconsciously, immediately after the acquisition of the house, to "invent" a Christmas tree which, like the manger, connected grown-ups and children. At the very threshold of our life together, Napanoch allowed Ray and me to dream of a new family. The identification of a tree in our forest, the day-long transformation of that tree into the symbol of a moment in our childhood within our Alpine village, seemed an answer to our yearning.

Twenty years after Ray's death, with our daughters scattered across three continents, the *humus* of the original myth has dissolved. My voyage to Africa suggests the first awareness of our change in its perception. I seem to slide one step at a time, without pain or nostalgia, from the past into the present. During my voyage from New York to Paris and Paris to Nairobi in 2009, as well as during my few days in Paris, I relive in my memory, with detachment and now without pain, moments of my past from the villas of my childhood in Merano. I recall the happy years I spent with Ray in Paris.

***

I lie on the blue sofa in my living room on Riverside Drive where I used to read *Anna Karenina* and Homer to Ray shortly before he died. Night is falling fast and early. The soft music from the record player lulls me into oblivion of the noisy world around me. It is strange to spend the weekend in New York instead of in Napanoch where Lavinia drives the family every weekend in every season, regardless of the weather. It had never happened for years to miss a December weekend in Napanoch. This year however, Michael is still working in China or Singapore or India and Lavinia is taken by her students during the day and by Fiamma and Tristan at home at night. Both her children and her students share a common problem: final exams. At home as usual, in the absence of Michael, Lavinia is the leader of the pack.

December has become for us recently the most frantic month of the year and Christmas is a relief from the daily pressure.

A year after my African Christmas, I see Dony and her family in pictures. In one picture they sit under a tent in a national park observing the life of lions and zebras, when Lucas is suddenly frightened, Dony writes, by the sudden appearance of armed soldiers falling from the sky.

"This is Kenya today," she explains to her five-year-old son. "We try to bring peace to it, yet peace comes at a price."

***

The room slides slowly into darkness. Feelings and thoughts, hopelessly intertwined lead me to approach the forthcoming Winter Solstice 2010 within a world of memories of a faraway past.

In this strange world of fantastical memories, I see myself a little girl of six or seven plowing along in the snow on a winter night under a sky hung heavily with stars.

I'm walking home with my mother late in the evening from her last place of work through the charming alleys of our small town, among mysterious villas buried in parks. We walk towards what we call "Papa's Villa" though it is not a villa at all, just a modest, recently built, two-storey house where my brother and sisters wait for Mamma to feed them.

Mamma is as usual in a great hurry to get home. After Papa died suddenly one night when I was five and the "creditors" had deprived us of everything we owned, Mamma could only count on herself, her teaching and tutoring to support us. That kept her busy for many years building informal schools where she taught groups of adults after her classes at the regular public school. Her pupils were Germans mostly from Germany but, after a few years, also from Austria, and there seemed to be a special bond between them and Mamma. They loved us all and took turns in setting up Christmas trees for us even though many of them were Jews.

Mamma was in eternal motion, moving from one place of work to another. The epicenter of all her movements was of course her family—her four children—in whatever Villa she had placed them in different moments of their lives. When she entertained me, as a child, with a story she was never as relaxed as Papa, who truly enjoyed telling me stories. She was always doing or thinking of whatever she still had to do or where she had to be next, like on that particular evening when she was trying to get me to walk at her pace in the deep snow.

"Tonight," she said, "is the 21st of December. Something extra-ordinary is happening *up there,*" and she pointed up to the sky as if that 'something' had to happen then and there in front of our eyes. She did not specify that it actually happened every year on that same day.

Without looking at me, she continued with the air of authority that at times would freeze her students in their seats.

"Tonight, as we speak, *Sol Stat* which means the *Sun stands Still* for a moment until...."

I didn't hear the rest. I burst out crying, terrorized by fear that the 'something' happening to the Sun at this very moment, up there, in the sky, would have an immediate effect down here on earth.

Then suddenly something did happen down here on earth between my mother and me. She held me in her arms, taking my frozen hands into hers to warm them. Slowing down to my pace, she told me a marvelous story from one of the two books that Nonna Maria, my father's mother, had given to her when she was a young teacher in her Village, before she met Papa. According to Mamma, Nonna Maria, after whom I was named because Papa adored her, lived an unusual life for the village where she spent her summers and a good part of the rest of the year. She painted, read, and had great fun mingling with the villagers, telling them stories and capturing moments of their lives in her painting. When Mamma became a village teacher, Nonna Maria took a great liking to her and they spent time together every day in her sturdy mansion that looked like a castle. Mamma would read to Nonna Maria from books Nonna provided.

"These two poems," Mamma explained, "that I would read to Nonna Maria told of the innumerable adventures of some Wandering Knights of Old. Most of the time oblivious of the War, their Christian king, Charles the Great, fought against the 'Infidels' called 'Moors.' These marvelous Knights of Old, Christians and Moors together, rode happily day and night from clearing to clearing through the forests of Europe and Asia. They rode from one adventure to the next, inspired mostly by love."

Love for a woman, Mamma was quick to point out, which inspired faith in oneself, mainly in one's own instincts rather than in something one would read in books, like 'justice,' 'fortitude,' and what she called 'temperance.' "Goodness," she clarified, "means *being* good not writing books for others on how to be good."

"The best stories of these two books," Mamma told me, "are about duels inspired by an all-encompassing love for a most beautiful Princess that hailed from the Orient called Angelica. The two poems are as long as their authors wanted them to be because human instincts persist stubbornly in one's life and great Knights in Arms wandering through forests rarely die."

"Angelica didn't care for any of her innumerable suitors. She happily moved about by horseback from China to Paris and back, encountering marvelous 'adventures' of her own and most of the time escaping her suitors. What is worse, she indiscriminately used for her own purposes whichever of the noble warriors she met during her voyages, without ever giving an inch of herself to any of them. Why? Simply because she did not love any of those great and noble warriors. Finally, she meets a handsome young soldier by the name of Medoro who is wounded to death. She instinctively takes care of him and in so doing falls in love with him and marries him."

That marriage, as I understood it, broke the delicate balance of what Mamma called 'adventures.' Orlando, the greatest of all Christian warriors had so far carried out the greatest 'adventure' of all, always inspired by what Mamma called the 'folly of love' which she described as a kind of magic. When Orlando discovers that Angelica is actually in love with another man, a little pagan soldier, he loses faith in love, in life, in himself. He could have killed himself, but that never happened among these indefatigable knights. He plainly lost the power and force that so far had made him invincible.

In the very middle of the *Orlando Furioso* (*Orlando Insane*), Orlando, hero of the earlier poem *Orlando Innamorato* (*Orlando In Love*), loses his mind and turns into a gigantic beast gone mad. The cause of this change, according to Mamma, was not love but jealousy, which, according to her, counteracts the wonderful, vital effects of love.

By the time Mamma got to that point in the story we had reached home, much to my regret. That was the end of it. At least for her. Not for me. From that night on, I kept stalking her in her endless movement, trying to find out what happened to

Orlando after, as she put it, he had lost his mind. Mamma smiled and kept postponing. I couldn't believe that such an exciting story would end with its hero reduced to a brute.

On a beautiful quiet Sunday in spring, long after that memorable Winter Solstice, while Mamma was resting with all of us children after a long walk among flowers in the clearings of our forests, I discovered what happened to Orlando. King Charles the Great was the one in the story who suffered the most from the loss of the very best Paladin of his court and army. In despair he turned to God for help and God couldn't avoid helping him. It was in his very best interest since King Charles the Great of France was the defender of the Faith. God revealed to the King where he could recover Orlando's brain. Mamma then told us the wonderful adventure of the English warrior Astolfo who is ordered by his king to go to the Moon to pick up, among the other objects that man discards on earth as useless, the big flask containing Orlando's brain. Forced to inhale his brain and thus restored to mental sanity, Orlando quickly regains his original French valor of which the Italian poets had deprived him when he had crossed the Alps from France to Italy. He forgets about Angelica and, in his full, primitive vigor, wins the final duel against his enemy counterpart.

The night of December 21, 1927, Mamma gave me precise directions on how to interpret the Winter Solstice. Walking home in the snow, she reassured me that what happened to the sun during the Winter Solstice was a normal phenomenon in the mysterious life of the heavens.

"Instead of worrying about it, we should celebrate as we actually do at Christmas. December 21 is the shortest day of the year. From tomorrow on light will triumph a bit more every day. Through ice storms or snowstorms nothing will stop the days from getting longer until...the trees will bloom, the birds will sing, and we will pick flowers again together in the meadows of our mountains."

That was then. Another time. Another country. Another world. Today, as I walk home on December 21, my eyes are fixed on the glowing globe that enlightens Columbia's campus walk below the Rotunda. A huge golden ball hangs over the quiet Hudson from a wide sky. It shines into the living room, from my three windows open to the River, as if to call for human attention.

That moon on the Hudson instinctively becomes an obsession, and I can no longer wrest the glowing planet from its poetic depth and history. Words become the warf and warp of life. I fall back into trying to measure mortal time, like planetary rotations, through poetic meter. The grounded, recognizable recurrence of natural phenomena bestow upon us the gift of memory. And remembering is living, the distillation of pain.

O graziosa luna, io mi rammento
Che, or volge l'anno, sovra questo colle
Io venia pien d'angoscia a rimirarti: e
tu pendevi allor su quella selva
Siccome or fai, che tutta la rischiari.
Ma nebuloso e tremulo dal pianto che
mi sorgea sul ciglio, alle mie luci il tuo
volto apparia, che travagliosa Era mia
vita: ed è, né cangia stile, O mia
diletta luna. E pur mi giova
La ricordanza, e il noverar l'etate
Del mio dolore. Oh come grato occorre
nel tempo giovanil, quando ancor lungo
la speme e breve ha la memoria il corso,
Il rimembrar delle passate cose,
Ancor che triste, e che l'affanno duri!
(Leopardi)

O graceful moon, I can remember, now
The year has turned, how, filled with anguish, I
came here to this hill to gaze at you,
And you were hanging then above those woods
The way you do now, lighting everything.
But your face was cloudy,

swimming in my eyes, due to the tears
that filled them, for my life
was torment, and it is, it doesn't change,
beloved moon of mine.
And yet it helps me, thinking back, reliving
the time of my unhappiness.
Oh in youth when hope has a long road ahead
and the way of memory is short,
How sweet it is remembering what happened
Though it was sad, and though the pain endures!
(transl. Jonathan Galassi)

Later that night, as I lie in my bed near the window, unable to sleep, my mind's eye draws back to that motionless globe hanging over the Hudson. Ariosto rises in my dreamlike state, his quiet writing, year after year, his octave upon octave of adventures by wandering knights, paradigmatic of man's courage against the hateful firearm that Orlando eventually buries in the Ocean after having killed its owner in a superb duel with his sword called Durindana. While Ariosto's knights wander from Europe into Asia, into mythical Africa and across mysterious Atlantic islands, around the poet Ariosto the Italian peninsula is being destroyed in a war between Spain with its artillery and France with its heroic cavalry. The Duke who hired Ariosto to compose poetry for him was a lover of firearms. He owned two cannons, the *Diavolo* (Devil) and the *Terremoto* (Earthquake), and he spent his days on the battlefield.

I wonder at times if the Duke of Este would not have preferred to have at his service a tense, nervous writer like Machiavelli who, in near-by Florence, got into serious trouble for his excessive love of action, whereas Ariosto, in Ferrara, was peacefully wandering about in his imagination. Ariosto, who instinctively disliked Machiavelli, reacted to the cruel world around him through irony, by inventing a most intricate combination of adventures for Charlemagne's Christian Paladins and the Moors. This must have been the textual solution for otherwise insoluble problems that he discovered and that he grounded in a world of his own creation.

After allowing his knights for over two thirds of his poem to wander the world, the poet Ariosto felt the urge to find a solution to his convoluted stories of the mythical war between Christians and Muslims. This had to be, of course, a Christian victory. In the reality of facts, the Peace of Cateau Cambrésis in 1559 solved the problem for a great part of Europe. In the reality of the imagination, however, the solution comes from the moon, probably a full moon that mesmerized the poet from his quiet little home in Ferrara.

It is that very Moon that obsesses me tonight, that ultimate measurer of time that glows timelessly over both shores of the Hudson.

Beautiful Barbuda—my Little Africa and its African Roots

My winter has been harsh and interminable. By the official arrival of Spring on March 22nd in Napanoch, we still walked from the car to the house on a thick block of ice. New York had avoided the snow, but icy winds hit the city day in and day out, blowing straight from the Arctic through the corridor of the Hudson. Michael's sudden announcement of a week to be spent by the family on a very exclusive island in the sunny West Indies was greeted by all of us with a sigh of relief. I greeted it as a god-sent without knowing that Barbuda was to perform the miracle I needed.

Before leaving New York for the Caribbean, I had reread my journals and remained stunned by the enthusiasm I recognized in the diaries of my past African visits. I understood that what had discouraged me from evoking my latest visit to Africa with the freshness it deserved was the silence of a vast empty apartment in New York, a home that once echoed with the voices of children and adults, of students, projects, friends, books that lived once with me like human beings and now stood on long shelves, immobile, dusty objects. In particular, the joyful harmony that unfailingly concluded all disagreements or fights within the family. In this apartment we had lived as a family an intense life since the student riots of 1968. An old contorted and dried out trunk of a palm tree still reminds me of those days. You would not recognize it. It is what is left of the gift I gave you, Ray, on Palm Sunday, 1958. The rioting students in 1968 had hurled the plant down the stairs of the Mathematics Building when they discovered it in your office. Lucia had brought it back to life once we repossessed it.

My ignorance of the history of the island of Barbuda lifted it into the realm of magic. The name itself, *Barbuda*, evoked for me at first the ill-famed Ebuda in Canto VIII of Ariosto's *Orlando Furioso*, a little island of the poet's imagination tucked away in the foggy Ocean, where a horrid monster devoured all shipwrecked Irish damsels.

A beam of light had hit me while still in New York—its source, the magic yarn of a man of the sea, a certain Captain Marlow who penetrates the darkest heart of Africa inspired by an unreachable Kurtz. When packing for Barbuda, I took with me Conrad's *Heart of Darkness.*

As we landed in Antigua, we fell prisoners to a fluctuating mass of travelers. Everyone but us appeared to know where they wanted to go. The five of us, Fiamma, Tristan, Lavinia, Ingrid, and myself huddled near Michael who, as usual, towered over the crowd. Then a little man, dressed in white, caught sight of us and quietly led us out of the crowded main airport into a little private area where a gentle dove took us under its wings. Just the six of us, nobody else. For twenty minutes we flew between two strips of blue, the sea and the sky. Then we landed smoothly on a thin strip of pink sand between two lines of tall coconut palm trees, their branches softly waving in the noon breeze. Barbuda greeted us, a magic island between sea and sky.

Two athletic young men approached us with a smile that said "Welcome to our island, we are happy to share it with you as long as you help us to keep it." There was something about those two welcomers so direct and honest, genuine and generous yet proud and defiant, that left me wondering what kind of people lived on that island which, from the sky, had seemed to me a swampy wilderness hardly surfacing from the intense blue of the sea. I discovered later that the island was a coral plateau, as wild and poor now as when it was 'discovered' in the seventeenth century. I discovered also the next morning, in Codrington, its only town, that Barbuda had been, since the end of the seventeenth century, 'home' to a group of handsome and proud Africans, 'placed' on it by a British nobleman, Admiral of the West Indies.

To my surprise during the week of our stay, as I lived quietly within my family around the lodge, between the alley of the palms and the sea, Antigua hazily surfacing on the horizon, Barbuda unconsciously became my *little Africa*. In its natural and human beauty, it surfaced like Venus from the sea, a bit at a time, day after day. The lodge and its environment throbbing with 'indigenous' life offered me a vision of a deserted island that comes to life by the hard-coordinated work of a group of tightly-knit families. I thought of Mamma's Village.

The black families of Barbuda had made the island their own home since the moment they walked on it three centuries ago as slaves. Some way, somehow, the best of Africa in appearance and substance had found a way to survive and to thrive on a poor deserted island of the Caribbean, after being transported there by the hurricane of human evil that was slavery. In the twenty-first century, from the combined perspective of nature and history, Barbuda then became for me an 'island' of Africa made of sky and sea, in uninterrupted dialogue with the continent. In a mysterious way, I surmised, a group of Africans must have conquered their independence not through bloody revolts, after years of slavery, but immediately upon arrival in the New World by virtue of their physical and moral beauty and an irrepressible love of freedom that they still expressed today in their looks and behavior.

What I discovered on my own was that the Admiral had passed on the property to his family for years on end and that the people of Barbuda still see the Codringtons as their Founding Fathers, England as their second home, and English as their language. As for the American Kelly who owned and operated the lodge we lived in, he built a Foundation that would allow the islanders to profit from his 'adventure' forever in the world of the twentieth century and beyond.

On my last evening in Barbuda Lavinia and I walked back alone to our cabins from the main building, under the usual dark blue sky so thickly woven with stars as to make me long for the African skies I had not long before enjoyed with Dony in Africa. We were both silent, afraid to break the magic of the evening. At the height of our cabins we stopped. We could not take our eyes off that sky, "as blue," Lavinia whispered to me, "as the background of our manger in Napanoch."

After a moment of silence: "that blue," she added "is the background of miracles."

***

Napanoch, July 22, 2011—your birthday

My dear Ray,

In my letter to you on Palm Sunday I told you how Barbuda had fired my imagination. I now dream of those fierce and handsome Barbudans—women and men gathered in the Anglican Church of the village of Codrington, preaching and singing the glories of motherhood and families.... It keeps surfacing as a vision strangely tied to my visions of Africa and to *Mamma in her Village*.

Ingrid, who inherited your analytic intelligence, showed up for Memorial Day dinner with her usual exquisite home-made cake and the print-out of the last chapter of a book by Michael Wood, *In Search of England: Journeys into the English Past*. In its closing chapter, "An English Family," I discovered what a British noble family, as nominal owners of the island, had contributed over two centuries towards making the inhabitants of Barbuda the deciding element for Kelly to choose Barbuda as one of the best sea resorts in America.

For Wood, England had always contributed the highest moral values of civilization wherever in the world it pitched its tents. In the case of Barbuda, Wood concludes, the future of the island was set by the decisions and consequent directives given by the founder of the "Codrington dynasty," the Admiral Christopher Codrington, Governor of the Lewards Islands at the end of the eighteenth century, after he had received the lease of the small, uninhabited, desolate island of Barbuda "for the value of one sheep," if requested. He was inspired in his decisions by the group of slaves that he had bought fresh from Africa. Tall, extraordinarily handsome and healthy, women, men, and children alike without distinction, those 'slaves' were members of tightly-knit families. Codrington realized before he bought them that he should not break the bond that held together their society. Therefore, he firmly established, as the basic rule that his family respected over the following 200 years, never to break up a family and to always feed and care for those slaves as partners in the colonization of the island. He treated them like his workers back in Bath; they were seen as free English citizens, members of the Anglican Church to which the Codringtons belonged, a church that stood by them throughout the two centuries. This is why the Barbudans, Michael Wood argues, wherever they live as emigrants, mainly England but also Canada and New York, regularly return to their island as 'home' to celebrate there with 'Codrington Parties.' They are proud of the English language they speak and treasured their British citizenship as long as they could. By the time the abolition of slavery came along in 1834, the Barbudans were officially the owners of an island that had been for two centuries their own.

Wood's invaluable contribution to my understanding of life in Barbuda for two centuries preceding 1834 and immediately after that was his highlighting the sale by public auction in December 1990 of the "Codrington papers" by Sir Simon Codrington, who was forced to sell everything he owned in the midst of a difficult divorce.

Those papers proved to be as important as the founding of the Codrington Library by the founder of the family, Christopher Codrington, in All Souls College in Oxford. They witness that for two centuries Codrington's descendants kept careful track, on a daily basis, of all information concerning each one of their slaves as if they were citizens of Barbuda.

I ran through Wood's last chapter, excited that the Codrington Papers had allowed us to establish the place of origin of those African slaves who, by their own look of quiet self-determination, had conquered their original masters: they hailed from a village north of Accra on the Gold Coast, infamous for having furnished to America thousands of slaves.

Grateful to Barbuda for having given me the vision of a corner of Africa whose sons had conquered their masters, I considered my recent African experience not as a newcomer to the continent, but as one who had visited Africa four times before 2009. I had done it hand in hand with Dony. It had been an unforgettable experience for a mother who took personal interest in the adventures of her daughters after they had flown the coop. You remember, Ray, how I flew to Peshawar, abandoning you, sick in New York, and my work at Columbia? You so wanted me to go to Dony, sad you could not follow me.

Now, as in the Past, it was real human beings that spurred me into action. I needed a piece of 'living Africa' on this side of the Ocean to lead me back to an Africa I had discovered, after your departure, step by step in the last decade of the twentieth century.

***

To call for Ray's presence among us at the distance of twenty-one years from his death seems preposterous, though he was indeed with us in 1994 when the whole family enjoyed Christmas together through three unique safaris that, centering in Nairobi, familiarized us with three different aspects of the Rift Valley.

Unfortunately, memory tires with age, like eyesight and hearing. The longer I live the more I am convinced of this sad fact. The spark to revive the past comes from the present. Yet only the past allows me the excitement and vision to enjoy the present. My problem continues to be how to reach the present, which is in itself incomprehensible for me if not accessed and grasped through a richer and fuller past. What I long for today is to enrich the memory of the Africa I am about to visit with the vivid memory of the Africa I enjoyed a few years after Ray's death from 1993 to 1995. My memory at first reacted like a tired instrument. It was the experience of the island of Barbuda, one of the pearls of the resplendent necklaces of the Antilles, that opened the palace of memory.

I could not explain how my tired memory reacquired the strength to revive my past African experience so it could surface in all its intensity to feed my recent African Present. Yet when I came back from the island of Barbuda to my peaceful, dull corner of Riverside, the exciting Africa that I had discovered and enjoyed with Dony, those diaries of 1993-94 and 1995, came to light as 'Present' through a revived, vibrant, living Memory.

The experience of my past combined with my most recent visit to Africa relived through Barbuda allowed me to visualize and accept the concept of a family in movement, as it spreads and develops beyond its natural habitat, adapting to new environments, a family's movement through the lens of history.

***

February 13, 2012

My dear Ray,

Yesterday, Donatella, the child born in the best years of our lives, turned fifty. I remember going to the hospital twice with no results. She was born on my third visit. It took her time to come into this world. When I came home with her, we were received like a royal couple. She was, as her name suggests, a "little gift to the family."

The three girls we raised, each so different from the other, have built three different families in three different continents: Europe, America, and Africa. Yet each one draws inspiration as a working wife and mother from what she assimilated during the years she spent with us. Each one in her own way is the heir of her education in New York, Napanoch, and across the Atlantic.

As I look at Dony today celebrating her birthday on vacation in South Africa with her husband John and her seven-year-old son Lucas, I can hardly recognize the wandering knight of yesterday who had opened Africa to me at the end of the past century. What happened to that little girl of once who, as a three-year-old in Ankara, Turkey, had begged Lucia to take her back to Napanoch, to the *Casa della Neve*, the House of the Snow? I see Lavinia and Donatella in their childhood and early adolescence sleeping together in a wide sunny room in our old apartment on the Upper Drive. Lavinia who had trouble falling asleep would ask Dony to chat with her, but Dony would refuse to be interrupted in the "stories she was telling herself." She was daydreaming, adding to the stories I used to tell her.... Dony was always a dreamer who loved the intimacy of the family but absented herself up the mountain, in the orchard, perhaps on a tree where we couldn't discover her, leaving the chores to her sister Lavinia. As a lover of stories, Dony was an early and avid reader. Before I realized it, she had moved from Dr. Seuss to Mary Renaud.

Donatella is the one who went beyond the Europe of her parents into an altogether new world. I see this as the result of the love that inspired us in our so-called educational project. There was actually no project, no plan, no special idea we followed in raising our girls, no books we read on the subject, no discussion we held between ourselves or with our friends. We both disregarded or were disinterested in 'education' per se as a discipline of study. We had no interest in Teachers College and its latest experiments. Having chosen the *Lycée Français* by chance in 1958, we held on to it because it did not in any way interfere with us as parents. The school provided a well-thought-out program while we involved our girls in our own life, as we lived it, having them follow us wherever we went, on all the projects in which we were involved.

Our "educational method" implied at times physical inconveniences for the family. Our 1965 year-long exploration of the Mediterranean from Gibraltar to Istanbul and Ankara, when Dony was three, Lavinia eight, and Claudia sixteen, is still remembered in the family today for Lavinia's acute appendicitis in Athens on August 15. Rome became famous for my month-long stay at the *Salvator Mundi* hospital near our home on the Gianicolo. I lay in that hospital almost lifeless for a month, sustained by blood transfusions after a miraculous operation for a perforated ulcer with peritonitis. The operation was performed by the only surgeon working in that hospital, a certain Dr.

Stefanini who, according to my Columbia colleagues, is still famous for his superb technique. My recovery took place in the company of the family in a villa in Capri where our host, Giuseppe Sansone, a colleague in our CISE courses, decided to publish my critical edition of Lorenzo Valla's *On Pleasure*.

In raising our girls what mattered most was a closeness to them that allowed us to interact constructively with each other as we did with the people we met on the other shore of the Ocean, colleagues who would eventually end up teaching courses at Barnard and Columbia and participating in dinner parties with Lucia's lasagne at home. Our family's European excursions were diligently prepared at home in Napanoch. A week-long family exploration of Sicily carried out by invitation of Paolo Emilio Taviani at the time Ministro del Mezzogiorno, while I was Director of the then Casa Italiana, was diligently researched by our teenage daughters Lavinia and Donatella so as to submit a report to their class. Once in Sicily, however, they spent most of their time in between visits to archeological sites eating crates upon crates of blood oranges provided by our handsome young driver, Vincenzo, with whom they had both fallen in love.

What our girls discovered between 1963 and 1990 beyond their home in New York and Napanoch was a world of European cities and villages which before the advent of the highways were connected by often unpaved roads. Crossing the Atlantic, year after year, on ships and then planes, allowed our new family to become acquainted with extraordinary people on the other shore, men and women so enthusiastically open to receiving us as to encourage Ray and me to invite them back as our partners in New York.

Settling in

I made sure all was packed away safely along with my passport,
health-card and traveler's checks. Our manger was to be placed
under our Christmas tree in Africa.

When the pilot announced we were about to land in Nairobi,
two-year-old Fiamma, standing up on her seat against all rules
was singing her own Christmas song: "I see Dony in Africa."

After the usual long sweaty lines, Dony holds Fiamma and
me in her arms. We wait in the balmy tropical night a whole
hour to obtain our nine pieces of baggage.

Although exhausted by twenty hours of travelling and a
gruesome three weeks at least of heavy work in New York in
order to make it, the enthusiasm of the family knows no
boundaries.

"Watch out for the baboons." "Do they bite?" "No, they
don't, but..." That *but* introduces two-year-old Fiamma to the
mysteries of Africa.

Now I see the two sitting in a corner. "Here," Dony leads
Fiamma by the hand, "you'll light the Christmas tree for us."
Michael is called upon to solve the last electrical problem.
Electricity, how it works or doesn't, is part of the African
mystery.

The tree shines in the dark. It is a small, dark green tree,
artificial of course, perfectly symmetrical. Fiamma turns to me
for help. Together we dig around in my precious brown bag.

175

"Jesus's mamma," Fiamma complains, "got more hurt on the trip."

"Yes, she did," I agree, "but we can still make her kneel near her baby." Under the Christmas tree there is a hut with a thatched roof and, on a side, a long crocodile. Fiamma places little Jesus, taped to his crib, as far away as possible from the crocodile. She is also worried for the safety of the two white sheep and the three-legged dog. Dony insists on keeping the crocodile where he is. We come to a compromise. We'll place our superb dromedary, carrying one of the three kings, between Jesus' family and the hungry crocodile. Three pine cones from the Catskills also help to raise a definite barrier between Jesus and the crocodile.

A half-moon lights our way through the garden down to the guest house over the swimming pool, where three members of the New York family settle under an immense white mosquito net in a room that looks onto the dark African night. Birds call from the banana trees. And darkness envelops us. Back in the house, Dony puts out all lights. In my room of last year I open the window. The fragrance of jasmines sweetly envelops me as I fall asleep.

Among cascades of flowers and green we reach the giraffes, a quiet enclave of meadows, trees and huts where the table of ecological rules is readable on every wall. A quiet, softly smiling African woman distributes cereal to feed the animals. Most of the children are shy or afraid. Fiamma has learned fast how to place the little balls of cereal at the very tip of the giraffes' long, raspy tongues.

Thin and tiny, with small narrow eyes and a bright smile, a woman jockey who is very much pregnant, Alex Peterson, spreads a blanket on the grass under a huge tree to serve us tea. We wander under the banana trees and the cactuses, some immense, some contorted, some straight like candelabra, some with flowers, some with thorns. Interspersed among the cactuses and embracing them are gigantic trees: a rain of flowers, green, purple, blue....

Through an empty, sun-drenched Nairobi, past the tenements and the cemetery, on a bumpy road we reach the estate of Karen Blixen. If it weren't for the tropical trees and the N'gong Hills on the horizon instead of snowy mountains, we could think we were in Switzerland.

Kenya's legendary past holds on with a quiet lunch at the old restaurant, *The Horseman,* a wooden building buried under flowers of all sorts. On the veranda two journalists and their children share the meal with us, the Belidas of *Voice of America* and *Deutsche Welle.* Together we end the afternoon at the Horse Races, under fantastic islands of white clouds sailing overhead.

It is 7 a.m. The table on the chilly green veranda is rapidly emptied of piles of eggs, toast, and tropical fruit. Today being "malaria day," those who take Lariam swallow their pill.

By the swimming pool the world around us has lost its identity. The map says it is Africa. It could be the moon or earthly paradise. The intense experience of yesterday dissolves into the thin turquoise air of today.

The city lives at a distance from Muthaiga's paradise that is cloaked in green: the white skyscrapers, silhouettes against the blue, the crowded avenues with beautiful names, the long lines of slim Africans walking lightly along them, the crowded market beyond the imposing mosque, the N'gwezi Masai market on the hill, the Indian shops, the "African heritage," the money changers, the begging children, the colorful Somalis: Nairobi hits us with its strange identity made of bits and pieces, a mosaic that is not easy to decipher, a fluid puzzle, a cauldron of people that have been brought together too recently to allow the city a clear identity. To each his own.

At the New York Times Office in the PS building, the first skyscraper of Nairobi, Dony's staff, Hanna and Hanson, embrace us all. The Indian ladies in saris at the well-protected jewelry shop downstairs efficiently change money for us while the vendors at the market try to deceive us with gentle malice and the peddlers pursue us with a disarming albeit annoying intensity. Fiamma is shuffled from the arms of one family member to another. Dony explains, protects, leads, warning us constantly of the dangers of being misled. She is our true guide, at least for now.

In a society where the "rich" are separated from the "poor" with a clearly marked distinction, there is an in-between special class called "tourists." Do we belong to that class? Our identity in Kenya, we hope, will come with time, experience, and happy coincidences.

At dusk, we move out from home, having changed clothes, to get our share of the Nairobi Christmas parties. At the American Embassy, under an ample tent, one hundred and fifty Americans and friends crowd in the garden of an estate. Vinnie looks for milk to calm a whimpering Fiamma, but milk proves to be a difficult item to find at an American Christmas party in Nairobi. With a tall, blond, handsome consul we talk about Peshawar and the Mujahedin, about the refugees from Sudan and Somalia. Asia and Africa melt under a dark blue sky studded with stars.

On rocky roads we move on to the Pakistani Embassy. The ambassador's wife receives us with open arms among the flowers at the entrance. She is tall, robust, lively, full of fun. Fiamma needs milk. Vinnie is sick with nausea. We are all tired. Yet, after five minutes in the warm company of dark-eyed diplomats, writers, and artists of Pakistan and their mellow wives and daughters in overflowing veils, we all feel perfectly at home because the sharp insight of problems in the world today are such a stimulus to the conversation with our Pakistani hosts and their friends that instantaneously our family becomes part of another wider family.

Having broken down the barriers of our close family, we all experience an elation rarely felt today. Ethnic conflict, the inadequacy of the United Nations to hold back the world's overflowing rivers, the inadequacy of democracy to look straight and courageously into the thousand faces of poverty, the incompetence of diplomacy, the lack of political leadership, the many painful issues that are constantly present within the wider family of humanity but of which we rarely speak in the close family circle become connected with new spiritual ties. We are happy together because we can open our hearts to each other, those who came from the West and the East, the South and the North, in agreement and disagreement. We search for possible solutions to what does not have any solution in sight.

Like death and war, these problems are with us to stay. The delicious food, personally prepared by Madame l'Ambassadeur, and the excellent wine strongly contribute to the genial mood of the evening. Fiamma is peacefully sleeping on a sofa among colorful oriental cushions. The ambassador's daughter has found plenty of milk for her. The wide room is rather modestly furnished, its walls show here and there visible signs of decay. Yet the humanity of our hosts creates an ambiance of lusciousness, an oasis of tropical vegetation in a desert. Africa is all around us, yet only a small part of our lives and the world.

"Tonight, we light our Christmas tree together," the handsome Pakistani ambassador to Somalia joyfully announces, shaking a mane of long white hair, swinging his black cloak of light wool as he glides from one group to another and lifts a glass of champagne.

On December 20 my American family has reached the point of exhaustion. The world around us begins to lose its extraordinary attraction. Between the N'gwezi Masai market and the tea at the Norfolk Hotel we lose the bit of strength that we still had. At the hotel, we look at each other across the table blindly, yet Dony implacably leads us to the next step, fortunately a quiet spot in the suburbs. We are going to visit a slim, middle-aged English lady in whose luscious garden we deposit a sleepy Fiamma.

Today the family went food shopping while I lived two hours of serenity among the flowers and butterflies of the garden. When they return, I realize immediately that the magic of yesterday had dissolved. At 3 p.m. the sun hits hard over the hill where the N'gwezi Masai display their merchandise once a week. A tourist attraction, but today there are almost no tourists. Piles of colorful necklaces, carved wooden animals, ornaments of all sorts, fabrics of all kinds are on display, laid out on the dried-out strands of grass. The N'gwezi Masai themselves—head shaved, ear lobes cut adorned with rings, wide black eyes staring at us from small thin faces—add to the intensity of the colors on display with their red cloaks and checkered tunics. We mingle with them and listen, blinded by the sun, overwhelmed by the heat, to words that we do not understand. They come to life as human beings, however, because we comply with the function they expect from us: to bargain and to buy—that is to crown the bargaining with an acquisition of a precious color that will be translated by us from that dry hill burnt by the sun into an apartment in New York. Tea at the Norfolk, staring emptily at one another in utter exhaustion. Tea again in a garden in the suburbs among palm trees, the sun setting over the N'gong Hills, revives us. Vicky, a white Kenyan, makes necklaces with beads she collects from all over East Africa. She translates her "white African" experience into necklaces of old silver and turquoise, purple or Chinese red, old Venetian glass and golden, fossilized amber picked among the nomads.

We sip tea from antique English cups with cookies baked by Vicky's cook, old Ezekiel. A cool breeze relieves us. For Vicky, the British white Kenyan, Nairobi is home. I think of Dony's loneliness, a bird forced to fly on and on without a branch in sight on which to rest. Fiamma sleeps on the manicured grass of Vicky's lawn covered with an old, hand-knitted shawl. As we drive home, the moon rises in a pale blue sky. We are all silent. We light our artificial Christmas tree in silence: thin, small, cold, insignificant for us who live among the trees of the Napanoch forest, yet for Fiamma in Nairobi, who silently removes the crocodile from the manger, true to life. Dony and Michael are in the kitchen cooking a dinner of giant shrimps. Wine helps to cheer us up.

After Fiamma and her parents disappear in the dark grove that separates their home from ours, I try to talk with Dony. But there isn't much to say. She turns on the television and on a Kenyan channel we watch a movie: the life of Sophia Loren, straight from the Napoli ghetto into the limelight of Cinecittà.

On December 21 Claudia and Charles land from Paris, an injection of magic. On our way to the airport on a crispy, sunny morning, beggars dangerously intrude in between the cars stopped at a red light, trying to sell us, among other objects, paintings of white blonde madonnas with child. We are close to celebrating our Christmas.

Today Africa is home for us. Dony's friend Don appears, a tall, slim, and eloquent young man who seems to be in love not only with Africa but with its "discoverers," who happen to be all Englishmen like himself. Maps in hand, Don allows us to dream while sitting among the flowers of Dony's veranda. He unravels for us three lively voyages that will unveil the mysteries of Africa and…of a *Christmas tree* on December 24 in the very heart of Africa.

I know that Africa for us is being together in harmony.

***

The family was set to spend Christmas Eve in N'gwezi Masai land. I had read so much about the N'gwezi Masai that unfortunately I had almost lost that curiosity that makes you look forward to something. In fact, I had unconsciously confined them a bit to the kingdom of the imagination.

The N'gwezi Masai, according to Conrad, are "savage and superb, wild-eyed and magnificent." Blixen contributed to the general admiration: "A N'gwezi Masai warrior is a fine sight... daring and wildly fantastical... the muscles of their necks swell in a particular sinister fashion, like the neck of an angry cobra, the male leopard and the fighting bull and the thickness is so plainly an indication of virility that it stands for a declaration of war to all the world." Shiva Naipaul explains that "almost every trait of the N'gwezi Masai lent itself to a panegyric: their physique (tall and slim), the hematic regularity of their features, their nomadism, their militaristic code, their history of conquest and their predatory relationship with neighboring tribes like the Kikuyu, their steadfast resistance to the arts and habits of modern civilization, even their diet of milk and blood was a contributing factor."[3]

On the map the Masai Land seemed reasonably reachable. We are not a family of explorers whose blood churns at the thought of moving into the unknown. We are in a way primitive—realistic, that is. Wherever we go we tend to feel at home and feel able to cope with what we meet. We do not "expect," we tend to take in what life offers us. In this case, the N'gwezi Masai Mara on Christmas Eve, implied, for me at least, some kind of a Christmas tree.

Of course, I also knew enough about the Kikuyu to enjoy the company of our driver Simeon during the long stretch to reach the Mara.

---

[3] *North and South*, Penguin: 1978:53

The Kikuyu, we knew, having lived for a long time closer to the Europeans, enjoy the reputation of having betrayed their own customs by assimilating European ways, thus acquiring a hybrid behavior which makes them less "admirable" to us. They do not enjoy the reputation of "primitives," whatever that means.

In the superb organization planned by Dony and Don for our expedition to the N'gwezi Masai Mara through the challenging approach that descends from the Nairobi plateau and crosses the stretch of the Rift Valley, we were assigned to the car driven by Simeon who turned out to be the most amusing, annoying, and informative companion and guide we could ever have dreamt of.

Simeon is 56 years old, has four children, all grown up and successful. He is half N'gwezi Masai and half Kikuyu. His father, a N'gwezi Masai, took a Kikuyu wife. Somebody had told us that the N'gwezi Masai often take Kikuyu wives because their own women are run down and made sterile from venereal diseases which of course they get from their men. Simeon has a fine, well-chiseled, ebony face, a small nose, a perfectly designed mouth which opens rarely into a smile of shining white teeth. Simeon is at first silent, but, sitting near him, I try my best to make him play guide and host. He warms up and provides us with information on the land, the customs, himself, the N'gwezi Masai, mostly about the car we have the pleasure of sharing. One of his front teeth was extracted at age twelve as part of a Masai ritual ceremony. Rituals are good.

We cross Nairobi driving south through estates drowned in flowers. I had read and heard from Dony and seen with my own eyes that the Highland was a natural place to settle for the Europeans, a kind of Switzerland in the heart of Africa. Favorable climate, good-natured Kikuyu, fertile soil, plenty of sun and water. It was easy for the White to give in to the temptation to recreate Europe in Africa. Besides, Africa offered what was denied in Europe: wide spaces, virgin forests, wild animals. A room for dreams out of which, as Blixen wrote in the 1930's, a new nobility was born. The place literally provided the heraldry: "The lion stood straight up over it, dark, and behind him the sky all aflame."

At first my main worry was to make my driver understand that he should go a bit faster. He was driving at twenty miles per hour on a well-paved road for no apparent reason. I knew that in the car behind us, driven by Dony, the rest of the family was fidgeting. Simeon finally stopped among the eucalyptus pointing to the immense expanse of the Rift Valley, all homogeneously brown.

Simeon was not impermeable to the beauty of the landscape. His sparse, laconic observations revealed that he was as proud of those cascades of flowers over estates—plantations of coffee or tea— many now, Dony had told me, turned cooperatives, as the Europeans themselves. Of course, Simeon could not share the Europeans' dreams of overlordship, their feeling of going back to "primitiveness," that is to the beginning of the world which only Africa could provide. As a child, he had lived the Mau-Mau revolution, shared the Uhuru exhilaration with the Kenyatta people, witnessed the economic rebirth of Nairobi as the center of NGO besides tourism. All this was in his background. Now he could find a form of eloquence only when he talked of the corruption of President Moi and the present government. Nairobi suffered deeply from it. He owned a two storey-brick house in one of these Highland villages and was as proud of it as Alphonse the cook back home in Dony's estate.

Pointing to the immense expanse of the Rift Valley, "We cross it!" he exclaimed with pride. "Road now very bad!" Then he put on his brakes and, pointing to the last stretch of good paved road, said proudly "Italian war prisoners have made it. Also built church here." The church still stands, in good condition, lonely in the green, like all catholic churches in Kenya, as we'll find out. The catholics have the best schools and the best churches in the land. Simeon belongs to the Church of Christ. They celebrate Christmas with "rites." And rites are good for the people.

So far, along our descent into the Rift Valley, Africans had accompanied us, often walking in two straight lines alongside the highway between villages of brick houses with corrugated tin roofs. From the moment we begin the crossing, human beings appear only around the two villages. White clouds navigating majestically through an immense blue sky are our only companions or distraction for hours on end. Once in a while a flock with a shepherd, a young boy cloaked in red.

Suddenly, the road deteriorates. A light central streak of the old asphalt carefully avoided by the few carts that navigate it with us is flanked by two formerly paved ruts scarred with craters of all sizes. The few cars that come by carefully avoid the central hump and so do we. Dony's car behind us shakes like ours, half hidden in a cloud of dust.

"Why are we going so fast?" I ask. They honk. Since my direct appeal to Simeon to slow down serves no purpose, I try conversing with him. On both sides of the road for miles on end wire fences enclose long expanses of flat, reddish-brown pastureland. "To whom does this land belong?" I ask.

"European farms," Simeon replies and, seeing my interest, he repeats in a matter of fact tone at regular intervals "more European farms." Europe has moved into Kenya. Being ignorant of Kenya's economy, I would like to know if Europeans are welcome in Kenya.

Simeon is slowing down. This however worsens the ride. We hit each pothole head on.

"Only Europeans!" Simeon asserts with complacency.
"Is that bad?" I ask.

"Oh no!" he reassures me "Kikuyu could not have it."

"What about the N'gwezi Masai?"

He laughs heartily. "Oh no, not the N'gwezi Masai!"

All of a sudden, the car leans almost perpendicularly to one side. One of the very few cars on the road has taken to the left of the median, bouncing triumphantly from pothole to pothole in a thick cloud of dust. It cuts us off. A European driver would have cursed. An Italian driver would have made obscene gestures, a sufficient cause for both drivers to stop and cover each other with insults. Our Kikuyu-N'gwezi Masai driver laughs heartily and with a sudden jerk recalibrates his car, straightens it back into position, and launches it at good speed behind the culprit, bouncing happily along.

By now we have completely lost sight of Donatella's car. "Couldn't these Europeans who own half of Kenya fix the road?" I ask in despair. "Oh no, no," Simeon declares emphatically. "No, this is for our government and the government, *our government*," he stressed in disgust, "is very, very, very corrupt."

The car has slowed down to the point that we could hear each other's voices, while Simeon proudly lists the examples of corruption of his government. Suddenly Simeon stops the listening and the car.

"We have lost Donatella," he declares in the same tone in which he had identified the owners of the farms. "We must go back."

With a sudden jerk he turns the car around, settles it properly on the other side of the road and begins retracing our steps. Ten minutes without seeing anybody, jolting from one pothole to the next between deserted European farms, flat lands without a single tree, the sun gliding in and out of white clouds. Finally, we spot Dony's car parked on a side of the road. Simeon is on fire. One of her tires is torn to shreds. Before we know it, he has changed into a mechanic. Dressed in overalls, he and Michael are under the car. The repair work, they say, is going to be long.

The road stretches endlessly, a grey ribbon scattered with red spots, the potholes. The European farms spread endlessly on both sides of the road up to the horizon: grayish-red with a few flowers. There are no herds or shepherds to be seen. A few men and boys in red tunics materialize out of nowhere to check out our mechanics. Dony remains with the men. Claudia, Lavinia, Charles, with Fiamma in his arms, and I wander beyond the fence. The landscape is deadly silent. The immense sky, detached from the earth, speaks a language understandable perhaps by the wide-winged eagles or vultures that once in a while sail by, gently carried by the wind. It speaks through the clouds, white and fluffy, unreachable, boats with white sails, planes with white wings, castles with white turrets, white cities that dissolve into white immense statues of gods and goddesses, white soft fluid ideas, quickly replaced by others. White sailing in the bluest blue. A divine marriage of white brides with the blue that embraces them.... White dreams carved out of the blue.

The work for Dony's car completed, we settle back into the two cars. Did Simeon learn his lesson? We are back to the bounce and shake, Claudia vigilant this time that we not lose sight of Dony's car. The "European farms" yield to more modest "farms" with thin roofs and stucco walls announcing a village.

A "town," Simeon corrects me.

"The capital of the N'gwezi Masai, Narok, could be a great capital if it weren't for the corrupt government which makes sure that nobody has a chance. Kikuyu and N'gwezi Masai alike, suffer from a common misery because of the government."

The gas station of Narok in the midst of the Rift Valley is a meeting point for the few tourist cars that, like ours, have ventured to reach the N'gwezi Masai Mara by land, the hard way. We visit the advertised clean bathrooms. A horde of N'gwezi Masai surrounds us. Tall, very thin, small round heads, ear lobes pierced, what's left covered with earrings, red-flowing robes and tunics. Of course, they have something to sell us, but they do so unaggressively, almost as an invitation to get close to them.... Evidently, they are well accustomed to tourists, but in their isolation, tourists are more of a distraction than a prey.

Out of Narok a few miles of paved road, then, from pothole to pothole, we climb towards those hills that for hours on end had seemed unreachable.

No more fences, no more "Europeans." Hours in a desert of gigantic euphorbias, huge candelabra with thick cactus-like branches stretched symmetrically towards the sky, thick arms of green filled with well-protected water.

Suddenly the road ends. We are now softly rocking in a prairie of green-brown grass.

"How far are we from Don's camp?" I ask.

"Behind those hills. One hour," Simeon replies, pointing to a brownish line at the horizon.

The magic land of the gigantic euphorbias has yielded to a prairie scattered with acacias. We cross the first set of hills just to discover that there is another one on the horizon. "Are we still in the Rift Valley?" I ask Simeon, hoping he would say no.

"There you see Tanzania," he replies with satisfaction. Suddenly I feel alone, suspended in between a mysterious, unending, silent prairie, prey to a pitiless sun, and an unending blue sky which speaks through dancing white clouds.

I make one last attempt: "Simeon, how long yet before the camp?"

Simeon looks at me patiently and answers as usual.

"One hour. Behind those hills."

Then I let myself go to the sky, to those clouds that do not ask questions but allow themselves to be shaped and dissolved into sails and wings, castles and flying angels....

"A lion!" Simeon's joyful cry catches me at the threshold of a dream in which Africa had gently melted into an immense sky. Instead of a lion, screams from the other car greet the first flock of gazelles, graceful dancers of the prairie. Then, after a thicket, Simeon plunges our car down a rocky bank into a torrent and then climbs up the rocky bank on the other side. I am so worried about Dony's ability to handle this last piece of African bravura that I forget to hold on to the handle above my head. I fall on top of Simeon who looks at me puzzled: "I think we made a mistake," he says, "this is the wrong camp."

Behind the bushes lies a cluster of four dark green tents huddled together, with a wider tent looking over them. I hear behind me the ponderous breathing of Dony's car that rattles up the rocky bank.

Then I open the door of our car and fall into Don's arms. Dressed in colonial style, with khaki shorts over thin pale legs, a khaki shirt, a khaki hat, he greets me: "Welcome to the N'gwezi Masai Mara!" Twelve men in dark green uniforms stand behind him. What happens next belongs to another world.

In the Camp

The tents are nestled around the bushes, wrapped by the circling branch of a torrent. A central tent serves as restaurant; behind it, an improvised kitchen with a big open fire. The main tent opens onto another open fire pit. Our tents are set up at a lower level, one near the other. Each has a shower and a toilet in the back with water to be provided by Don's staff.

Don is sweet and gentle but deadly serious. He means what he says. After a quick cold meal, he allows us half hour to wash up. Then he packs us into two cars, freeing Dony from the responsibility of further driving. He uses his two cars and puts Daniel in charge of the afternoon exploration. From now on Daniel will be our spotter.

Daniel is a handsome twenty-seven-year-old N'gwezi Masai. Thin and agile like a wild animal. Daniel possesses the strange attractiveness of a mythical figure sprung from an Egyptian tomb. He gives us the feeling of a world with which we have nothing in common, a mysterious world of dances in the grass under an immense sky where white clouds sail or at times hang immobile over us. We were not born at the sources of the Nile; we did not migrate centuries ago with our cows from the Nile to the heart of black Africa; we did not wander for centuries in the high grass coexisting with the lions, the leopards, the elephants, the gazelles, the zebras, the impalas, the toupees. His ancestors did.

It is difficult to resist Daniel's charm. He is tall and handsome. He has fine features, chiselled out of ebony, beautiful hands, and a fascinating ivory smile. He had to walk twenty miles to come to work this morning. He did so without eating anything, just drinking a glass of milk. At lunch Don had introduced him to us with a legend. One of fifty-six children of a happy father, Daniel had been chosen by his tribe or clan to represent the N'gwezi Masai at a convention in Paris where he was received by President Mitterand. Refusing to take the metro when he wasn't driven around he enjoyed walking long distances alone. At the hotel where he lived he stunned the restaurant by asking for "a glass of blood." Actually, he did it on purpose because his folks in general very rarely drink blood. They do so not by killing a cow, but by slightly slitting a vein and letting the blood flow out, the quantity of blood they need.

As soon as we leave the tents, Daniel's world opens up bluntly. The savannah overwhelms us at first sight. We are not alone. One can spot cars like ours here and there all across the plain. Yet life in the prairie goes on undisturbed. The constant throughout are the gazelles who dance so lightly they do not seem to touch the ground, and the zebras whose large white and black stripes design the geometric component of the Mara. The zebras walk majestically, oscillating rhythmically, some a little pregnant, some very much so. The impalas contribute a geometrical dimension of their own with their high horns and painted stomachs. They like to watch over the prairie standing on top of hills, silhouetted against the sky. The jackals stick out of the high grass, their necks stretched. The hyena is a solitary apparition, out of a thicket, her maculated hair all rumpled.

Our spotter stands, binoculars in hand, overlooking the wide stage. He directs the driver: move left. We sail for a while through high grass and bushes. Dark clouds on the horizon. Silence around us. Further, further, orders our spotter. Claudia, Dony, and I are with him. The rest of the family follows in Simeon's car. I can hear at times, when we stop, Fiamma's happy screams in Charles' arms.... Where is Daniel taking us? We can see them now from far away. They are like specks at the horizon. Soon they walk towards us, ten, twenty, fifty elephants, entire families, all happy together with undulating bodies, undulating trunks, mamas with their babies. They move at a rhythm of their own, following a music of their own.... Daniel is visibly pleased when they surround our cars, swaying rhythmically, snorting as if to greet us.

Further, further we drive, and faster. The sky in the west is glowing red and orange. An African postcard. Daniel smiles his deceitfully childish smile.In a clearing, surrounded by bushes in the idyllic peace of a golden sunset six lion cubs play. Oblivious of our presence, they playfully paw at each other. Simeon's car catches up with us. This is not a film. It is reality. A reality with which Daniel and his people have coexisted for ages and which does not belong to us. After night falls the lioness will deliver to them fresh killed gazelles or a zebra. Now in the golden sunset, the cubs play peacefully while gazelles, zebras, and impalas pasture a few yards away, calmly, as in Earthly Paradise.

A pale slice of moon hangs above our camp by the time we get back. A fire has been lit. Don, who has a very bad cold, invites us to join him. He opens a bottle of Chianti and places it on a set with colorful dishes and shining glasses.

Night falls rapidly while we eat an exquisitely prepared European meal. Our attention is taken by Don who, using two cereal boxes as props, illustrates the birth of Africa. This Africa that looks so compact on the map and so powerfully solid while we crossed it today by car screeches and falls apart and coagulates again in Don's forceful presentation. The Rift Valley with its European farms, its unending sequence of hills that we conquered one by one in Simeon's car, its majestic euphorbias lifting their turgid arms against the sky, is swallowed by brutal earthquakes. It vanishes into far away ages, lost in the darkness of time. Over us a velvety sky lights up with myriads of stars, the same stars that shine over our little house in the far away Catskills.

The fire crackles, creating circles of light that do not reach down to our tents near the water. Three tall, very slim N'gwezi Masai cloaked in red tunics take their places near the fire, their long, thin spear in hand. They will watch over us during the night. The stars, the wine, the N'gwezi Masai, the lions and the gazelles....

It is December 23. I sit in front of the tent at 2 p.m. The sun would be unbearable if it weren't for a gentle breeze. After lunch, to relieve us from the fatigue, all the girls with Charles gather in our tent to sing Christmas carols. *O little town of Bethlehem, O*

Tannenbaum.... The wind sweeps our words away onto the savannah.

At dawn this morning two of Don's boys woke us up and brought us water to wash. The day was so pure I felt its innocence in my bones.

We sail in the high grass, as the day warms up, with two spotters, Daniel and our old friend Simeon. Gazelles fly like birds in the high grass. The horizon darkens with grey clouds. Against them three acacia trees stretch their skinny arms. Under a very pale blue sky the golden green becomes a sea of grass.

Two N'gwezi Masai young men wrapped in red tunic ride with us. They communicate with us through their ivory smiles and their laughter. Daniel tells us they are "young warriors." Does this mean they don't guard cows anymore? Yes, they just hang around the village. Clearly, we all agree, the N'gwezi Masai have their own version of Fellini's *vitelloni*, their "loafers", as well. They are expected to fight the lions or 'enemy tribes.' In practice, they steal their neighbors' cattle.

The sky is now painted a stunning grey and pink. A herd of impalas flies by, their male marching proudly in the midst of many females and their babies. We have lost sight of the other car. A flock of ostriches crosses in front of us. They walk unperturbed on their long, thin legs like the legs of the N'gwezi Masai. All around us animals graze peacefully near one another, zebras, impalas, gazelles, toupees. They dance lightly, as if skirting the grass. An eagle lingers above us. A herd of zebras gallops by, drawing black and white stripes in the grass. Gazelles graze at a standstill. Daniel stops the car to allow us to witness the birth of a baby gazelle. Free of its mother, it wobbles onto its legs, venturing its first steps. The sky is now crystal clear. Reflected on the sea of grass, it becomes a golden yellow.

Suddenly out of the bushes, totally oblivious of our presence, a solitary lion lifts his head and shakes his mane. A pinkish body is lying near him, almost covered by the grass. After a long pause what looks like a dead animal raises its head. It is the lioness he has conquered, Daniel explains, fighting against the two lions who rest, invisible to us, in the high grass not far from where we have stopped.

Our earthly paradise witnesses birth and death as well as sex....

The two defeated lions show up suddenly, their hair rumpled. From a thick bush we hear a noise. The head of another lioness fills a hole in the green thicket, then she drags out her body heavy with cubs. She walks towards the victorious lion, but he turns away from her. Daniel explains that lions make love for days, then they move on. It is the lioness who will take care of the cubs, hunting for them. We too move on, silently, in the high grass. And the prairie silently takes in the burning sun.

"Just take a big breath," Don's dinner story begins "and try to imagine...." Here is a little Scottish boy, putting his freshly washed clothing away in his suitcase. He is ready to face Africa.

We take in the story of Livingston and Stanley along with the excellent salmon, the tender roast beef, *pommes de terre à la française*. Tonight, we have French wine and a special cake. Fiamma is quiet in her mother's arms. She is finally falling asleep. Charles raises his eyes once in a while from his dish. We shall find out on New Year's Eve, at 3,500 meters in the Aberdare Mountains, after an almost equally luxurious European meal, the effect the Livingston-Stanley story had on him.

At nine everybody disappears into their tents in the bushes. The oil lamps burn vigilant in front of each tent when Claudia and I reach our own abode after having paid a visit to the "kitchen" and its staff. The way these thin gentle boys in green uniform every night produce a "European meal" worthy of the best restaurant in Paris, London, Rome or New York puzzles us.

They receive us around 'their' fire, while they eat their meal talking among themselves in their tongue.

"How do you manage to keep such an excellent staff?" we ask Don.

"I keep them happily working. Around us there is almost total unemployment."

It takes time to develop an inner sensitivity to a place that lives a life of its own, to avoid taking it as a huge natural zoological garden which it definitely is not.

As I awaken on December 24, I am overwhelmed by the immense, breathtaking peace of the Mara. The animals are silent. The grass is silent. The sky is silent. The world we live in silently takes in the powerful sun. Birth, life, death. We have come to watch the show on the stage of the Mara. The show is varied yet pretty much the same for all. The ingredients are the same. The result of their mix varies.

Gazelles melt in the grass. A N'gwezi Masai village stands out, a cluster of square mud huts surrounded by a stretch of manure where, I assume, the cows are kept. The unbearable stench stays with us after the village disappears from sight.

We drive for what looks like an interminable stretch of time through high grass until we reach a river. Brown and muddy, it flows between high grassy banks. The sun hits us pitilessly.

The hippos soon make their appearance first as huge brown bubbles, then with their heads, then finally with their full body, swimming along, brown on brown....

Not far, in an idyllic, cozy thicket close to the river, we watch, this time from the safety of our cars, a few huge crocodiles sunning themselves and some huge hippos swimming ponderously yet listlessly in the muddy water.

Silence here and everywhere. Here and in the ocean of tawny grass we cross to reach our camp. A herd of impalas, guided by a male proud of his high crown, crosses in front of us. The babies trot after their mothers, herds of them. *Antica pace?* Terrestrial paradise? Perhaps. War and death lurk around the corner.

Then Don takes us for a walk. The earth is parched, the grass very dry. No flowers. One scrawny plant becomes the object of Don's explanations: it looks like an eggplant; it is poisonous; it is resistant; it goes back to prehistory. What makes it unique is its capacity to survive.

Then, standing like a king over the wild stretch of the wide Mara, Don announces that he is about to cut the Christmas Tree.

He stops in front of a dead thorn tree, pulls out his knife and proceeds to cut off one of its branches. We carry the branch back to the camp. Its contorted shape evidences its barenness, its sterility. Life reduced to its quintessence. The bones of the earth. The skeleton of humanity. Its language is silence.

It was with a great effort that we dragged our pine tree from the heart of the thick forest in the Catskills down to the house in Napanoch. That effort was for our children part of the fun. The needles pricked and stung. Yet to be stung was inevitable, given the bulk of the tree. The richness of its branches, the perfect cone-shaped magic of its existence kindled our admiration. To place that huge green miracle in the heart of our living room in front of a crackling fire while outside forests and meadows rested in the white fable of a snowy blanket was an essential part of the rite of Christmas.

That was our Christmas.

The decoration was a song of victory: "We got you, magic forest, into our house. You are with us to stay for the rest of the winter, until, under the melting snow, the first daffodils will pierce the ground."

The manger nestled under the tree looked so small that at times we created another one on a table near the tree so that the children could play when they got up in the morning with the shepherds and the three kings. We even created Herod to revive the drama in full. Nazareth and Bethlehem coexisted peacefully with Napanoch and nearby New York as Ray, surrounded by all of his women, played on the piano the songs that expressed our peaceful coexistence within the wilderness.

At 5 pm, with the heat unbearably hovering over its wide expanse, the Mara is a radically different world. We follow Don along a narrow path in the grass as he effortlessly lifts the branch of the dead thorn tree high above his shoulders. Contorted and naked against the pale blue sky, it looks more like a cross than a tree.

Back at camp we decorate it with the little colorful ornaments that the British Vicky in Nairobi, who strung African necklaces with old European glass and pearls, had given Don for our "Christmas rite."

On the evening of December 24, the sky is set for celebration and for song. Burning red and orange, melting into yellow and violet streaks, an isolated acacia tree, a dead thorn tree. Daniel the spotter sings us a magical story from his mother. His large black eyes are fixed on the purple embers. I only half hear his singing. My mind wanders with the clouds, unable to settle on the branches of the thorn bush set up so dangerously close to the fire. Then we all sit around the resplendent table set for a delicious dinner, ending with a plum pudding concocted by Don from a unique British recipe.

Night falls abruptly over our tents, over our little world of cooks and waiters, over Daniel and the N'gwezi Masai, over Fiamma and Charles and the rest of my children, over Don who shared Africa with us. A night of myriads of stars, a world of stars without number, so distant that their sparkle takes eons to reach us.

The naked branch of our thorn tree projects a long protective shadow over our tents. Everybody in my family sleeps. We are all exhausted I guess, ready to give ourselves up to a silence without lights or to a silence that harbors lights of its own like the sun at dawn.

The next day, the twelve members of the staff stand in one line with Don in their midst, sending us off. Although we still have a wide stretch of empty Mara to cross to get back to Nairobi, I feel as if we left Africa in late December 1994 without even scratching its surface. It takes us three hours to reach Nairobi, this time on a different road, a "civilized" road. A gazelle bounds weightlessly on the prairie. Four leggy giraffes munch indifferently from an acacia tree. Under its green canopy a young impala sees the light of day.

I think back on the N'gwezi Masai village, the tall skinny women, their heads shaved, shining in the sun, their ear lobes heavy with ornaments, their long thin necks adorned with coiled wires, their dark shiny nakedness wrapped around the ankles by a purple cloth. They surround the car, aggressively exacting that we buy their colorful necklaces.

The vegetation changes: lelechua trees and more acacias. Safari cars on the horizon raise clouds of dust. Baboons venture so close to our cars that Simeon has to chase them away. For a while the vegetation gets drier and thinner until we find ourselves crossing a desert scattered with clusters of palm trees and bushes.

Back through the European farms on a bumpy road, climbing up from the Rift Valley into the highlands, we are drowned by avalanches of fuchsia bougainvillea. By the time we reach Muthaiga Crescent we had seen enough Christmas around the churches in the villages surrounding the city, swarming with people in pastel organza. We are happy to lock the gate behind us and dive into our turquoise pool. That evening we light our little artificial Nairobi Christmas tree and sing our Christmas carols.

The Mara lies far from us. Life moves on at great speed. Tomorrow is Dony's great Christmas party and then we are off again, this time going north, to the Equator, the desert of Samburu near the border of Southern Sudan and Somalia, and then to the Aberdare Mountains and a farm under Mount Kenya.

On Christmas Day, a big cloud covers the horizon. Fiamma has a high fever. While we prepare for the party her mother carries her around in her arms like a dead willow branch. We realize now that when Fiamma is sick the world darkens, the sun rises and sets without our noticing. Yet the party at Dony's home must go on. At 2:30 our adorable landlords, Stella and Ezekiel, show up with their cheerful friend John from upstairs. Their presence is a comfort and a guarantee that everything will be alright. The tables are set in the veranda. We are worried about Fiamma. We all think of malaria and of other tropical illnesses suggested by our fertile imagination and that everyone had warned us about. One of the first guests to arrive is the top administrator of the Aga Khan Hospital. As soon as Vicky introduces him to me, I lead him to Lavinia who is wandering about the garden and the veranda, with her little Flame half spent, hanging on to her as life support. He will accompany them to his hospital.

I can hardly wait while I move around the guests, my mind elsewhere, for this to take place. The party goes on with Dony's journalist friends, gentle and relaxed, as usual, on these occasions. Journalists are used to the sudden unexpected.

The Africa we had lived with the Masai is far away, confined behind the walls of the villa's garden, a dark presence with mysterious implications we did not take into account perhaps.

The Christmas Party at Dony's house in Nairobi is made out of expatriates of a special kind, most of them "observers" of Africa, some coming from Europe for a change of scenery.

We do not talk of Africa directly. Indirectly, I feel Africa as a kind of thorn in my flesh, a subtle wound whose cause I cannot identify. Why did we expose little Fiamma to all of this? How could we be so irresponsible?

On the other hand, I cannot help but feel proud of Dony who moves around the Christmas guests at her house with her most charming smile, her eyes shining. There is something that keeps Dony sane in all the shocking experiences to which she has been subjected in Africa. Is it her innate curiosity, her love for life, a life she wants to suck up stubbornly and relentlessly? In what way does Africa hit Dony? She is the one who opened up the continent to us as a family. Without her, Africa would still be for us a big chunk of colors on the map and some horror stories read in the press. Because of Dony Africa has become for us a complex entity made out of suffering humanity, idiocy, conflicting human interests, a mesh of conflicting internal interests, with interests interfering from the outside world. Interests from all sides.

I realize it now as I see her moving with her usual energy from guest to guest and I overhear her tell them why we came to Africa— not for a diversion from our daily routines but to challenge our beliefs, be shocked and confused, better realize what it means for us to be together, and for her to be with us. The guests come and go. The sun sets behind the overflowing canopies of green. The moon rises, myriads of stars unobserved by us pierce a velvety sky over our secluded paradise. While I look at Dony and look through her glasses, darkly I begin to see my Africa.

***

Travelling together as a family always played an important role for both Ray and myself in our married life from 1951 to 1990. With time, however, after Ray's death I realized that the deep motivation of that family voyage through Africa was not the same as the impulses behind our original ocean crossings.

In our 1994 African Christmas each of us was free and open to share a new experience with the other, in fact anxious to do so. Dony's invitation had come at a propitious time for all. Dony was at home in Africa, Michael was still searching for the job of his life, and I was in the midst of presenting to Columbia and to Italy the finished product with which they had entrusted me— the Italian Academy for Advanced Studies in America located in the fully restored and refurbished old Casa Italiana. The family visit was like a play in which each member acted out his or her role with the same spontaneity and enthusiasm as in our traditional Napanoch Christmas.

The Meaning of Christmas

Now, Ray, five years after we have laid your tired body to rest in a corner of our rural cemetery, I would like to light a Christmas tree in each of the three continents where my three daughters live: America, Europe, Africa. It comes as a blessing to me, an act full of joyful mystery, that by common agreement we decided to light this year our Christmas tree in Africa.

Nobody knew what our Africa would be like. I now know what it is not. It is not the dark continent that attracts the attention of scholars of all kinds, or retired couples or widows in search of the distraction of an animal-rich safari, or of lost souls who, having tried all Asian gurus, turn as the last resort to the primitiveness of the bush natives, or of those souls who generously give themselves to the idea of a new freedom for those who had been enslaved. Nor the Africa that arouses intermittently the interest of the West because of its internecine wars, its mass murders, the unbelievable corruption of many of its leaders; nor the Africa of the dusty Rift Valley where our far ancestor Lucy roamed freely; nor the Africa of Livingston and Stanley and their successors; nor the Africa that boasts an incredible wealth of minerals, the highest rate of childbirth or of infant mortality; nor the mysterious Africa that stretches through an immense, rapidly advancing desert into vast savannahs and thick forests; nor the Africa of snowy Kenya and Kilimanjaro; nor the Africa of Baroness Blixen; nor even the Africa of roaring lions, kept at a distance from pasturing herds by red-clad children of the N'gwezi Masai, of herds of stampeding elephants, of flocks of dancing gazelles, impalas and howling hyenas, of sleek leopards, sleepy crocodiles, and heavy hippos. Perhaps yes, a bit of all this. Our Africa was this and much, much more. It offered a whole continent for my family to light its new Christmas tree, the heir of the Tannenbaum that shone with its burning candles once in a corner of my Alps and for many years in a peaceful corner of the Catskills. Africa from now on was offering us its Christmas tree to make it our own.

***

The Ray who died to this world in 1990 was still with us in 1994 not as he was in the first family adventure to Europe in 1958 with one-year old Lavinia and nine year-old Claudia, but rather as he was in the last family voyage he took with us to Turkey in 1987. Old, tired, crushed by the remedies with which medicine allowed him to still walk and talk, he accompanied us a couple of years before he died through a long journey in Turkey which included the ruins of Troy. He never complained. He simply informed us with a frail voice when his body could not take it: "No, I cannot do that." In Chios, he had laughed at our misadventures in the dark of night, with Michael at the wheel through the wild island. He had rejoiced with us when we finally discovered a rundown Renaissance Venetian castle where we had to climb an interminable set of stairs to reach our apartment. We spent an intense week in Chios on dark volcanic beaches lapped by an ancient Mediterranean. This spirit followed us to Africa in 1994.

As for me I did not participate in this African voyage as I had, both as leader and follower, in our many transatlantic crossings of the past. From the moment we touched the soil of Africa, the continent imposed on us its own rules and regulations. I followed whatever our youngest, Donatella, had wisely planned.

***

Last night, December 24, 2011, Lavinia, Michael, Fiamma, Tristan, and I just made it to reach our mountain with enough daylight to cut and drag the "Magic Tree" out of the forest. I was allowed to attend the ceremony notwithstanding my age, always watched upon benevolently by Lavinia so as to avoid accidents.... Fiamma and Tristan who remembered me leading them from early childhood on in this expedition, bluntly requested that, in spite of my years, I should accompany them with flashlights down the steep road to the brook and into the forest to collect the moss, stones, acorns, rocks, and branches for the creation of the manger. Back in the living room, while they all labored hard under the pressure of time to set the scene for the 'miracle,' I sat quietly and watched from a corner, at a safe distance from all activity. I picked up a recent commentary on the Gospels, diving into the Gospel of Mark, the most ancient and thus presumably the closest to Jesus' real story.

Of all the four Gospel writers Mark is the one who clearly stresses that to follow Jesus one had to abandon one's family, to forget entirely about it. I was shocked by Mark's stubborn insistence. I fumbled to find a justification for it. Mark's details suggested to me that it would have been difficult for a visionary like Jesus to accomplish his vision while sticking to an old-fashioned family of five brothers all working with their father and an indefinite number of sisters wandering about the house.

That evening, as my contribution to our Napanoch Christmas, I ensured that, after Lavinia's feast, we all sit around the piano to sing all the hymns we had sung through the years. We sang together in a room free of gifts. Then we called Dony in Nairobi. It was too late to call Claudia and Charles in Paris. They had adorned the apartment in the old Marais with pine branches and attended the magnificent Christmas Mass in the nearby Church of Les Blancs Manteaux. We relaxed together while Michael, relieved of his old responsibility of backstage Baby Jesus and master of ceremonies, rested on the sofa which had been moved in front of the fireplace to make room for Fiamma's and Tristan's manger, a village in Palestine or perhaps in the heart of the Alps…. Behind it, touching the ceiling, rose a huge blue spruce with just a touch of decoration.

That evening, Lavinia, Tristan, and Fiamma tucked me into bed with the best Christmas wish we could make to one another: Napanoch would always remain the nest Ray and I had once built where all members of the family can find peace and love while we still live on a little planet called "Earth."

The children of our children, no matter where they are, under what stars, still insist today in believing. What they believe in today is actually the miracle of family togetherness as a positive factor in their lives. And I continue to believe with them.

Behind the manger a sky stretches out, painted an intense blue, while outside our little house, from deep within a dark velvet sky, hang myriads of stars as shining Christmas ornaments and the crescent moon that we share at different moments of the day with Paris and Nairobi.

Our Christmas 'myth' is not to be explained through theological sources, but through what, over two millennia, it has offered the popular imagination. For our family, it is my imagination, enthusiastically embraced and implemented by Ray, my imaginative memories of the first and last Christmas

Tree of my childhood in the Dolomites. This is the real world surrounding me.

***

I am obsessed with trying to recapture the fleeting instant of the Past within my own American family in which the miracle of Christmas awed us with a meaning that surfaced year after year, beginning in 1963, and again in a quiet, serene way, as we celebrate it, Lavinia's family and I, in 2011.

The spark to revive the past comes from the present. Only the past can shed new light on the present, enrich it with a new dimension that we are slowly losing in today's world.

After the experience of Barbuda, I look back on my diaries that suddenly reflect shining flashes of life I had spent alone with Donatella between 1993 and 1995. Those were the central years of my directorship of the Italian Academy for Advanced Studies, an institution whose first idea I had dreamt of suddenly on April 28, 1988 and had then realized under the auspices of Columbia and Italy. It was through Dony, as the East Africa Bureau Chief for the New York Times, that, between March 1993 and December 1995, I entered the forbidden kingdom of the Queen of Saba, a shining page in the Renaissance literature courses I then offered at Columbia; that I lived the life of Nairobi when it was still a small city surrounded by luxurious villas in parks; that I shared with her and her friends the end of the Rwandan genocide.

Before Barbuda my old diaries sounded like flashes of light in a mystery I could not penetrate. Barbuda had fueled the adventures that, through Dony's eyes, had opened up a new world to me. Barbuda not only healed the wound of humiliation that had been inflicted on me by the Italian Academy's guarantors, who for purely political reasons, had forced Columbia to limit my directorship of the Academy to the first four years, but—far more importantly— alleviated and filled the emptiness, the unfathomable loneliness in which Ray's death had suddenly plunged me. Those years, from 1993 to 1995, coinciding with the years that followed the inauguration of the Italian Academy, had changed my life while, simultaneously, Donatella had opened Africa to me.

Africa had entered my world as a continent explored alongside the wandering knights, Donatella's foreign correspondent friends. It was an Africa that stunned me with its waving deserts, immense rivers, wild animals, but mostly with its people who would soon now celebrate their fiftieth anniversary of independence, with Dony and John sharing this moment with them.

***

What changes my perspective on my Africa of 2009 is more than the shadow of an incumbent death, as Petrarch notes,

> *la vita fugge e non s'arresta un 'ora*
> *e la morte vien dietro a gran giornate…*

(life flees and stops not for an hour
and death follows it with long days of military march.)

It is life itself in its imperceptible flow. It is the urgency of awareness, the catalyst of *voluptas.*

Dear Ray,

I finally realize it is time for me to conclude my story in line with its beginning: our love story. Like Ariosto at the end of *Orlando Furioso,* I like to imagine a welcoming crowd at the port waiting anxiously for the conclusion of my voyage.

I am satisfied at having been able to overcome the pain of your physical absence by writing the story of my life beginning with the life of my family in Italy, which you so admired, to the one of our own family across Gibraltar which has been and still is a comfort to me in the ups and downs of my life.

As I close our story, I understand the intense meaning of *Gibraltar* that Maria Corti, Annalisa Cima, and I envisaged and discussed together at the end of the past century when the idea of the book was conceived.

There are few dates in my life that are as significant for me as 1990. It was a thrilling year in history, especially in Europe that, having witnessed the fall of the Wall in Berlin, was finally reunited; peace with Russia was achieved and the United States was living one of the most worthy periods of its history. In the spring of 1989, you and I shared our last earthly journey on a train that took us from Warsaw to Budapest leaving us with the feeling that we were participating in that moment of reunification.

It was that same year that I retired from teaching as a professor at Barnard while the Provost of Columbia appointed me to chair a committee that would transform the old *Casa Italiana* into an *Italian Academy for Advanced Studies in America*. Unfortunately, the political landscape in which the budding Academy was steeped, shaped by professors and politicians, proved a difficult and painful environment that eventually led to my forced resignation. I would have been lost had I not been able to rely on the unity of the new family that you and I had created and nurtured.

Today at 97, I continue my personal dialogue with the united Europe not as I had earlier, as the leader of the Center for International Scholarly Exchange, but as an "Emerita" in the etymological meaning of the word. The deep disappointments I underwent during my years as Director of the Academy led me to a new way of expressing myself. They shaped "the novel" which I had contemplated so often in the past but had never had the chance, the free time, to craft. The transition from active life to contemplation and writing did not, however, catch me by surprise, as I had always written stories and I had always tried to make sense of the world through narrative. The Turkish author

Pamuk inspired and guided me practically, suggesting how the novel is born from the literal "transferal" of tangible into fictional reality.

It is the family that you and I built together as an intimate part of our own life that allowed and encouraged me to choose, over the years, the right path in my work, which then was transferred into the subject of my novel. In fact, the family today stands strong with me in our fortress at Columbia and in Napanoch, helping me to overcome any obstacle that from time to time seems unsurmountable.

The perpetual changes occurring around us in the United States are very unclear and of concern to me. I often think of what we achieved at Columbia and of the inspiration that lay at the foundation of the creation of the Center for International Scholarly Exchange and the Academy. Our dreams and ideas were based on principles very different from the social and political trends of today. Today it seems that America has forgotten its original spirit of nurturing collaboration and of creating opportunities. It was in that spirit that I functioned since 1948 when I landed in my new country of adoption as a young teacher of ancient literature. Today, however, we are suddenly forced to accept a "tyrant's" political system for a country that has been over the centuries a symbol of liberty and democracy.

For me, who came to America to build a life and a family when Eisenhower was becoming President of Columbia University, this uncertainty about the future of America causes me a painful dejection. I believe history today explains the advent of Hitler and Mussolini as political phenomena of a recent past, but, as far as we know, does not yet succeed in defining the advent of the movement which we are experiencing now. Instead of working towards building unity as we did between professors across the ocean, today's world is careening towards division and discord, oblivious of the pain that the Treaty of Yalta had caused Europe.

As an American I feel increasingly lost in a maze, searching for the personal strength and the political leadership that may guide us out of it. This feeling of loss and confusion is what leads me back to the night before your death which opens my contemplation.

As I remember that night, you Ray, pressured by my desperation as fearfully I faced your death, described what you were seeing: the splendor of a light which you explained as undefinable and therefore indescribable. It is with that moment that I identify the seed of this novel that focuses on a family built on the solid rock of our love.

I recall that faraway night when I tried to freeze time in order not to accept your departure by stopping the many clocks that during those first years of marriage you had collected. In all these years the clocks you loved so much have remained silent, but they are now ready to ring again through our united family that celebrates Easter in Napanoch with the arrival of fifty little chicks.

I embrace you as always with all my love.

EPILOGUE

Tu ne quaesieris - scire nefas - quem mihi, quem tibi
finem di dederint, Leuconoe, nec Babylonios
temptaris numeros. ut melius, quidquid erit, pati,
seu pluris hiemes, seu tribuit Iuppiter ultimam,
quae nunc oppositis debilitat pumicibus mare
Tyrrhenum. sapias, vina liques, et spatio brevi spem
longam reseces. dum loquimur, fugerit invida aetas:
carpe diem, quam minimum credula postero.
(Horace, Ode I.11)

("You should not seek—to know this is forbidden—what end the gods have given to me, which end to you, Leuconoe, nor should you try out Babylonian numbers. How much better to suffer whatever will be, whether Jupiter assigns us many winters, or whether this is the final one, that now the Tyrrhenian sea weakens with its opposing rocks. Be wise, strain the wine, and prune down long-term hope given our short time. While we are talking, envious time will have fled: pluck the day, trusting as little as possible to the future.")

***

The sun sets over the Hudson, its rays reaching deep into my beautiful living room, shining over the antique dutch marquetry furniture that Ray and I bought second hand on Third Avenue. The rooms once echoed with the voices and laughter of children and colleagues. Every piece of furniture around me holds a secret which, for many years, the family shared.

Today the rooms are silent, so silent as to lead me inadvertently into the intimate life Ray and I suffered and enjoyed together. Joy and pain, expectations and

211

disappointments, exaltation and despair. I relive miraculously, in one brief instant, the entirety of my three quarters of a century on a continent far beyond Gibraltar.

As I look back on each volume of this trilogy, I see a pattern that one can only recognize from the vantage point of having lived almost a century on this earth. *Mamma in her Village* takes place in a time of peace on the brink of War, in a Europe resting uneasily on the powder keg of the great nineteenth century empires, the Ottoman Empire, the Russian Empire, and the Austro-Hungarian Empire to which my family was born. My view of the world begins at the dawn of the twentieth century, more than one hundred years ago. It begins with my mother's sheep in a village safely cradled in an Alpine valley. I am born not far from that village, under the rosy-peaked Dolomites.

Beyond Gibraltar is a challenge we all face in life. It is my own fairy tale, but, I believe, a story we all harbor within us. Some of us perhaps may never unearth it. It finds its center at first in the Mediterranean, the throbbing heart of western civilization, the Mediterranean that Dante's Ulysses and so many since him, sailed across and beyond through the unknown waters of the Atlantic Ocean.

Today that very Mediterranean has become a lake of tears, strewn with drowned infants and hungry, desperate migrants who cannot find a shore on which to land. The era I have lived in, the twentieth century, has contaminated the twenty-first with the horror of the Fall of the Towers and the creation of an army of criminals posing as fighters of a new civilization.

No individual life is lived separate from that of its fellow humans. No individual lives outside the life of the polis, untouched by politics and by his natural environment. And so my story too, as it tells the story of my family across centuries, cultures, and continents, reflects profound political changes.

The radical difference between the first two volumes and the final one is the role war plays in them—as the first two stories are shaped and molded by a World War and the final one by the Cold War. The characters onstage in *Mamma in her Village* are born in moments of peace, amidst the fields and the Palace of the Bishop of Trento. *Beyond Gibraltar* presupposes World War I and delves deeply into World War II. Though both *Mamma in her Village* and *Beyond Gibraltar* are set off by war or dragged into it, both end in peace. The tapestry of *The Other Shore* is woven against the background of the Cold War and ends in the tension of a new and undefinable war.

My mother and father came together across class boundaries to build a family buttressed by love. As the most basic building block of a functioning society, the family becomes the subject of my trilogy. It is a family not confined by geography nor diminished by death; a family that reflects the borderless, inviting, and creative space of the mind. It is fed by the imagination, strengthened by culture and education, and enriched by colleagues and friends. Thus from the little village in the Alps by the torrent Adige, my family moved south to Rome under the urgency of Hitler's descent through Austria. By the River Tiber we weathered World War II, and after four years in war torn, bullet-pocked Italy, I crossed beyond Gibraltar as a war bride on a Liberty ship to reach New York City and Columbia University, the other shore. As I forged a new family with Ray on the shores of the Hudson River, I kept crossing the Atlantic, building bridges with the Europe we had each left behind for the "New World." Our girls grown and Ray having crossed forever over to The Other Shore, I embraced the ineluctable reality of the family's diaspora. *The Other Shore,* my final resting point on the estuary of the Hudson River, reflects the borderless family we have now become, every daughter on a separate continent yet rooted in togetherness through the Alpine ritual of the Christmas tree.

From a foamy torrent of the Alps to the Zambesi River and Victoria Falls, the world has opened up to monumental waves of families desperately crossing borders, braving the Mediterranean, towards a Europe they hope will save them. This is the Europe both Ray and I had left behind, each of us following a different World War, the same Europe with which we desperately wanted to forge bridges.

As I near one hundred years of age, I finally have reached the end of the journey I began at the dawn of the millennium. Facing a world once again fraught with violence, I am still convinced that the only way to survive is through nurturing the family, no matter on what continent or in what form, the unity created out of conscientious collaboration and premised on the deep love between the two partners who forged it.

With my health increasingly failing and my strength diminishing comes the necessity of ending my writing. I launched volume I and volume II with the feeling that there lay a *beyond* to them. The promise of the trilogy's title, *Beyond Gibraltar* has been kept. The family has reached the last *beyond* that I can envisage in my finite life. The story ends naturally, like the Hudson flows into its age-old canyon carved beneath the Atlantic. I can still watch the river's tides ebbing and flowing from my window while others keep moving beyond it.

I strangely feel, facing my unknown, my other shore, as I did when, for the first time, I touched the shores of New York, one of three war brides and hundreds of soldiers, the cargo of the Liberty Ship *General Muir*. In my mind's eye I see myself surrounded by GI's anxious to land. Today, as I look at the Hudson from my windows, I do not feel I want to land any more.

It is time for me to put down my pen which, with my arthritic fingers, becomes harder and harder to control. I wrote this trilogy for my family, the living and the dead, and for whoever else might want to read it. I did so for as long as I felt able, no matter how difficult and lonely it might prove, to transfer life around me into a world of its own, a world in which not only life, but dreaming of life still made sense to me. It has been a marvelous dream.

The death of my sister Bona, the last member of my family of origin, in February 2015, signaled the beginning of the end, when *Spes ultima dea* ("Hope, the last goddess") vanished, gradually, month after month, and my own world shrank suddenly to a view of the mouth of the Hudson from Riverside Drive and to corresponding with my family by email. I have reached a stage where the world around me has changed so much as to no longer be recognizable as my own. I have reached an age where solitude has become, slowly at first, and increasingly rapidly towards the end, isolation. More and more, I lean heavily, both for physical and emotional support, on the family that is closest to me. In this new moment of life I no longer participate. I internalize.

There is no Kesselring, there are no catacombs to escape from nor a valid human project to complete. What kept me writing beyond the second volume, what kept me exploring *The Other Shore,* was the joy of creating a world inspired by the real family wherever physically or metaphysically it might be.

***

Born and educated in a classical school in the Alto Adige-Südtirol between the two world wars, Maristella de Panizza Lorch earned a doctorate in classical philology in 1942 at the University of Rome with the Accademico d'Italia Professor Vincenzo Ussani, Sr.

After fifty years of teaching, she is Professor Emerita of Italian and Medieval and Renaissance Studies at Barnard College and Columbia University. Among her books: the critical edition of Lorenzo Valla's *De Voluptate* (1431-44), its English translation *On Pleasure*, the edition of Ziliolo Zilioli's *Michaelida* (1431), (a study of Renaissance Epicureanism), *A Defense of Life,* with the philosopher Ernesto Grassi, *Folly and Insanity in Renaissance Literature*, an interpretation of humanistic literature and chivalric poetry. Albert Rabil's four volume collection of essays on Renaissance Humanism was dedicated to her, "a catalyst among scholars," in recognition of her promotion of Medieval and Renaissance Studies in America.

Maristella Lorch is known at Columbia for her courses on Dante, Petrarch, Renaissance Humanism, Renaissance Theatre, Machiavelli and Ariosto; in Europe, particularly Italy and France, as an active promoter of international exchanges. She founded and directed the Center for Medieval and Renaissance Studies, the Center for Italian Studies, the Center for International Scholarly Exchange, and the Italian Academy for Advanced Studies in America at Columbia University (1991).

She founded La Scuola New York Guglielmo Marconi, was member of the Advisory Board of the Lycée Français de New York, Vice-President of EPIC (the fellowship of Emeriti Professors in Columbia), and a teaching faculty member in the M.A. in Liberal Arts Program at Columbia's Graduate School of Arts and Sciences.

Since 1996, as Founding Director Emerita of the Italian Academy for Advanced Studies, she worked at the trilogy *Beyond Gibraltar*, a fictionalized memoir or *récit d'initiation*, based on her Euro-American identity, while at the same time offering courses for adults on Dante, Homer, Virgil, and Ovid. The first volume of that trilogy, *Mamma in her Village*, was first published by Ruder Finn Press, N.Y., in 2005 (ISBN 1-932646-05-1). The second volume, *Beyond Gibraltar*, was first published in 2013 by Pegasus Press (ISBN 1-889818-94-4).

Maristella de Panizza Lorch is the mother of three daughters and the widow of the mathematician Edgar Raymond Lorch. She divides her time between her homes in New York City and in Napanoch, N.Y.

ABOUT TBR-BOOKS

TBR Books is a program of the Center for the Advancement of Languages, Education, and Communities. We publish researchers and practitioners who seek to engage diverse communities on topics related to education, languages, cultural history, and social initiatives. We translate our books in a variety of languages to further expand our impact. Become a member of TBR Books and receive complimentary access to all our books.

Maristella Lorch's *Beyond Gibraltar* Trilogy

Fabrice Jaumont and Kathleen Stein-Smith's *The Gift of Languages: Towards a Paradigm Shift in Foreign Language Education*

Jane Flatau Ross's *Two Centuries of French Education in New York*

Darcey Hale's *The Clarks of Willsborough Point* Series

Fabrice Jaumont's *The Bilingual Revolution: The Future of Education is in Two Languages*

Our books are available on our website and on all major online bookstores as paperback and e-book. Some of our books have been translated in Arabic, Chinese, English, French, German, Italian, Japanese, Polish, Russian, Spanish. For a listing of all books published by TBR Books, information on our series, or for our submission guidelines for authors, visit our website at

http://www.tbr-books.org

ABOUT CALEC

The Center for the Advancement of Languages, Education, and Communities is a nonprofit organization with a focus on multilingualism, cross-cultural understanding, and the dissemination of ideas. Our mission is to transform lives by helping linguistic communities create innovative programs, and by supporting parents and educators through research, publications, mentoring, and connections.

We have served multiple communities through our flagship programs which include:

TBR-Books, our publishing arm; which publishes research, essays, and case studies with a focus on innovative ideas for education, languages, and cultural development;

TheBilingualRevolution.info, an online platform which provides information, coaching, support to multilingual families seeking to create dual-language programs in schools;

NewYorkinFrench.net, an online platform which provides collaborative tools to support New York's Francophone community and the diversity of people who speak French.

We also support parents and educators interested in advancing languages, education, and communities. We participate in events and conferences that promote multilingualism and cultural development. We provide consulting for school leaders and educators who implement multilingual programs in their school. For more information and ways you can support our mission, visit our website,

http://www.calec.org.

221